JOHN'S STORY OF JESUS

COMPANION VOLUMES

Mark's Story of Jesus by Werner H. Kelber
Luke's Story of Jesus by O. C. Edwards, Jr.

JOHN'S STORY OF JESUS

Robert Kysar

FORTRESS PRESS   PHILADELPHIA

Library of Congress Cataloging in Publication Data

Kysar, Robert.
  John's story of Jesus.
    1. Bible. N.T. John—Criticism, interpretation, etc.
I. Title.
BS2615.2.K933 1984   226'.506   83-16537
ISBN 0-8006-1775-4

K472H83   Printed in the United States of America   1–1775

*Dedicated
to the memory of
Ralph Berringer
who first taught me
to allow a story to
tell itself*

Contents

Preface

The left hand needs the right hand, and the right the left. One might say that there are two "hands" at work in the study of the Gospel of John. The one hand takes as its primary concern the history of the blocks of material found in the Gospel. This hand also works to discover the historical setting in which these materials were written and preserved. The other hand works at a different sort of task. Its goal is to study the literary structure of the Gospel just as it stands in our New Testament. The interest in history and historical setting is not the primary focus, but rather such things as the plot line of the Gospel. Obviously these two approaches need one another. We cannot really probe the historical setting of the Gospel or analyze the way in which portions of the book came to appear the way they do unless we understand the basic story of the Gospel as a whole. But once having seen how the Gospel story "works," then the interested historian can go to the task of discovering what lies behind the Gospel.

The title of this book prepares the reader for the kind of approach taken here. This is a study designed to understand the structure of the story line of the Gospel of John. How does it flow? How are the sections interrelated? What makes it effective as a story? What are the subtle meanings in the Gospel plot that the author may have intended the readers to comprehend? The exclusiveness of the focus of this book does not mean that the more historical concerns are less important or ineffective. It only means that we have set for ourselves a single, manageable goal. While our subject is the narrative plot line of the Gospel of John, I do not pretend this work to be a "structural" analysis in the technical sense of that term. This work intends a far less technical study of the story line of the Gospel.

Throughout the following pages I have referred to the author of the Fourth Gospel as "John." This is not to be construed to mean that I have solved the vexing problem of the authorship of the Gospel in favor of John, the son of Zebedee, or for that matter any other John. The evangelist responsible for the form of the Gospel as it stands in the canon is lost in the darkness of anonymity. If I refer to that person as John, it is for the sake of convenience alone.

Still another clarification is necessary. I have written simply, "Jesus said . . . Jesus did . . .," and so forth. I want the reader to know, however, that these easy ways of describing the action of the Gospel do not mean that John at these points accurately reports the history of Jesus of Nazareth. The question of the historical Jesus within the narratives and discourses of the Fourth Gospel is fraught with monstrous difficulties. This book makes no pretense of distinguishing between what is the accurate reporting of Jesus' life and words and which are the words and actions attributed to Jesus by the early church. Instead, we will attend only to what the author of the book says of Jesus.

It is also necessary here to say a word with regard to the order of the Gospel of John. Scholars have often pointed out that the narrative flow of the Gospel is at several points rough and abrupt. Some then have proposed that the original order of the Gospel has been disrupted and what we have is not the order the evangelist originally gave to his work. Others have proposed that the Gospel as we know it is an unfinished piece of work. It may be, they suggest, the first draft which was to be revised, but alas never was. There is no denying that John's story of Jesus is rough at points. One may at times feel that something has been left out or that something has been inserted to spoil the flow of the narrative. Still, it must be asserted that the present order seems to have made sense to someone in the final stages of the composition of the Gospel. Whether it was the original writer, a reviser who added and adapted portions of the Gospel, or the earliest of the scribes who copied the manuscript, someone thought that this story we are about to retell was worthy of our attention and careful reading the way it is. And so we put to one side the questions of the disruption of the order of the Gospel to give our attention to understanding it as we have it before us.

Finally, I want to say that this analytical retelling of John's story of

Jesus is a modest effort to aid the work of the evangelist. There is a beauty and character to the Gospel itself which makes any effort to retell it seem puny. Rather, I would hope only to provide some keys that will help the reader encounter more directly the power of the story held within the pages of this Gospel.

Introduction: Beginnings

1:1–51

THE COSMIC BEGINNING (1:1–18)

Where shall we begin? Begin at the beginning! And so John does. His story of Jesus begins, "In the beginning." Stretching our minds beyond their capabilities, the evangelist invites us to conceive of that mysterious point beyond time which the book of Genesis simply calls "the beginning." The existence of the Christ-Word originates beyond the reach of the human mind. It is not a point in time before time; it is rather that awesome transcendent reality that stretches through time as well as before, after, and beyond it.

This is the only appropriate beginning point for the story of Jesus, thinks John. It is not the case that he wants simply to say that before there was a Jesus of Nazareth the Christ-Word (*Christos-Logos*) existed with God; surely he wants us to know that among other things. More importantly he wants us to know that this man Jesus, whose story he is about to narrate, has his origin beyond time and space, beyond history and geography. Jesus is none other than the Word of God, which is as eternal as God himself. With the phrase "in the beginning," John invites us to understand that the Christ of whom he speaks is the one present in creation and the one who makes possible a *new creation*. So important is the Jesus story that it marks the occasion of a re-creation—a transformation of the first creation of such magnitude that it can be spoken of only in terms of that first ordering out of the primordial chaos.

15

Two essential questions are woven in and out through the verses of this prologue to the Gospel: Who is Christ, and what does he do? From the beginning John asserts the Christ-Word was *with* God, and he *was* God. The language is intentionally paradoxical—the Christ-Word is distinct from God ("with") and yet synonymous with God ("was"). The question of the identity of the Jesus figure cannot easily be boxed and packaged. The reader begins the Gospel face to face with the mystery of the being of this revealer, Jesus, and she or he will wrestle with that mystery for still another twenty chapters.

Who this Jesus is merges with what he does. The Christ-Word is none other than the agent through whom God created all things (1:3). The Jesus story is not only about the one who occasions the re-creation of humans; he is also the one through whom creation itself was accomplished. Redemption and creation are not, therefore, separable acts of the divine but one continuous act. Creation is the beginning of redemption, and redemption the continuation of creation. But the continuity is present because of the centrality of the Christ-Word to both. John again stretches our minds as he asks us to realize that the Jesus whose story he is about to tell is one who began God's work in creation and now continues that work in the form of a single human being. 1:4 continues this theme as it calls the Christ-Word "Light" and the "Life of humans." The two titles are filled with overtones of creation and redemption. They are descriptions of what benefits the Christ-Word brings to humans. He brings these benefits precisely because he is none other than the divine light and life of the world.

John 1:5 introduces a further theme and one that is prominent in the subsequent verses of the prologue and the entire Gospel. The "Light of humans" shines in the darkness of sin and disobedience but is not subdued by them. The Greek word translated "overcome" can mean "being subdued." But it can also mean "comprehend" in the sense of understanding and appropriating. Perhaps John here intends for us to attribute both meanings to the word. The darkness of this world cannot comprehend the Christ-Word, so foreign is this world to the divine world. But neither can the darkness of this world extinguish the light. The terrible truth of the resistance of the world to divine light is a solemn point John will make again and again throughout the Gospel.

But now we are suddenly redirected by 1:6–8. This interlude in the prologue wants us to see that John, the Baptizer, is not the Light but a *witness* to the Light. In that simple statement we have nearly the whole of what John has to say about the Baptizer. The same message intrudes into the prologue again at v. 15. There the distinction between John and Jesus roots in what has been said of the Christ-Word in v. 1. Unlike Jesus, John is an ordinary man with a divine mission. In this singular message the evangelist anticipates what he has to say about the Baptizer as part of the "historical beginnings" of the Jesus story and about the Baptizer's later witness to Jesus (3:22–30).

Apparently John intended that we think of the Light that shines in the darkness as the presence of Christ in the created order. But now he clearly turns to the presence of the Word in the historical person, Jesus of Nazareth. Beginning with 1:9 and continuing through 1:11, John affirms that the Word was present in the world and among humans, but his presence was rejected. Even though he is the true light which can enable humans properly to comprehend their existence, he is not accepted. He is not "known"—known in the sense of received and appropriated in terms of our self-understanding. Even though he is responsible for our very existence, he is not received. And that is the tragic character of the whole of the Jesus story as John tells it—the tragedy of the human rejection of the divine Word. In introducing this theme of rejection John prepares us for the division between those who do accept him (the "we" of v. 14) and those who reject him—a division that appears on nearly every page of the Gospel.

John 1:12–14 affirms that some did accept him, however, and for them there is a power that relates them to their Creator. It is a power that makes humans into God's children. It is like a second birth, John tells us, but not a human birth. It is a birth bestowed by God upon those who recognize God's presence (what is described here as "glory"). That glory which is the very nature of the divine has now become human, and through this single human life we see the glory of God. 1:14 may be the hub around which the prologue revolves. It is an important verse carefully balanced with two thoughts. The *first* is that the Christ-Word became a human being, took on a fleshly, bodily existence, and "pitched his tent" in the midst of us. The divine Word is now a human who can be seen, touched, heard, and all the rest. Such a thought suggests that the Word is disguised, transformed from

its divine existence. The prologue would seem to want us to understand that the incarnation means that the Christ-Word is veiled as he
dwells in our midst. But lest we think that the Christ-Word is God
incognito—entirely hidden from us in his human existence—the *second* thought of v. 14 is added: The glory (the divine presence) can be
perceived in the incarnate Christ-Word. For those of faith the historical, human Jesus is one in whom God is found. In him we behold the
glory of God.

This description of the cosmic beginning of the Jesus story ends
with a rehearsal of the benefits of the "encampment" of the Christ-
Word in the world. The first benefit is that grace is piled upon grace
through Jesus. The benefit in relation to the Hebraic-Jewish tradition
is summarized with the claim that the Law came through Moses, but
the saving power of the grace and truth of God is brought through
Christ. This is an abstract point that John will make more concrete in
the Gospel proper, namely, that the Torah is indeed the revelation of
God, but Jesus is the further revelation which supersedes the Law.
But the thought of the prologue continues: One can only know
another person if the latter bares his or her soul. In Christ, John says,
the very "soul" of God is brought near to all humans. This is so
because Christ, the unique expression of God, comes from the "soul"
of God (1:18).

For the fourth evangelist, the beginning of the story of Jesus is in
the creation of the universe itself and, even further, in the relationship
of God and his Word. The story of Jesus that the evangelist will sketch
out for us is indeed a story of a human on the plane of history; but it is
at the same time the story of one who comes from beyond the world
and from the beginning of all existence.

THE HISTORICAL BEGINNING (1:19–51)

The beginning of Jesus is really "in the beginning with God," but
that is a prelude to another beginning. Throughout 1:1–18 we have
seen that the cosmic reality of the Christ-Word is already related to
the world. Christ came into the world, his light shines in the world, he
is rejected by the world, but he also drastically alters the lives of those
in the world who receive him. So it is not fair to divide 1:1–18 from
1:19–51, for the cosmic Christ-Word is not isolated from the world

and from history. Vv. 1–18 are not mere speculation but are rooted in a historical event. But now in 1:19–51 John paints the picture of the beginning of that historical event in some detail.

Here is John, the Baptizer, doing precisely what we have been told he would do. He is the signpost pointing away from himself to the one who brings salvation. When questioned about his identity, he claims only to be one who prepares the people for the appearance of the yet-hidden Christ. He does not want to claim any of the honorific titles for himself—Messiah, Elijah, or one of the prophets returned to life (1:19–21). Instead, he claims only to be that voice preparing the path for God's striding through our world—the voice Isaiah centuries earlier had spoken of as God was about to liberate the people of Israel from their bondage in exile (Isa. 40:3).

We have heard the declaration that John is not the light, but the witness to the light; we have overheard a conversation with the religious leaders in which the Baptizer makes no claim to be the Christ but only to be the "announcer" of God's arrival. Now we hear him specifically identify Jesus as the "Lamb of God" and the "Son of God" (1:29–34). The hiddenness of the Christ is now broken by the appearance of the figure of Jesus. Although John does not explicitly baptize Jesus, he claims to have witnessed the descent of the Spirit upon Christ. And with this description the Baptizer steps quietly from the stage of the drama John is unfolding for us. At a later time the Baptizer will again take a role in that drama (cf. 3:23).

The historical beginnings for the Jesus story involve the witness of the Baptizer to Jesus but also the gathering of those who will accompany Jesus in his ministry. The first of the disciples are recruited from among the followers of the Baptizer, one of whom is Andrew. He brings his brother, Simon, to Jesus, and Jesus gives him a new name befitting this new beginning in his life. He is Cephas—Peter. Then Philip is called to follow Jesus, and he seeks out Nathanael and invites him to join the newly formed family. In Nathanael's case, it takes a bit of convincing, but Jesus' strange words to Nathanael do convince him that this Jesus really is the Christ (1:35–51).

This story of the Baptizer's witness and the call of the disciples is an appropriate prelude to the Gospel as a whole for several reasons. First, there is a kind of "chain reaction" among those who have found Jesus. One is called, and he in turn calls another. The point the evangelist seems to want to introduce here is the function of witness; it is through *witness* that humans are led to recognize Jesus as the Christ. Here we have three different witnesses—the Baptizer, Andrew, and Philip. The human witness to Jesus is the catalyst for the occasion of encounter with Christ. This function of witnessing is part of the meaning of discipleship as it is sketched out in these verses. Notice the prominence of the word "follow." It appears no less than four times (vv. 37, 38, 40, and 43). Obviously it functions in this passage as a code word for discipleship.

Finally, note the use of titles for Jesus in this story: "Lamb of God" (vv. 29 and 36), "Rabbi" (v. 38), "Messiah" (v. 41), "the one of whom Moses and the prophets wrote" (v. 45), "teacher" (v. 49), "Son of God" (v. 49), "King of Israel" (v. 49), and—Jesus' own title for himself—"Son of Man" (v. 51). The evangelist emphasizes once more the question of who Jesus is. Here he is identified with a whole string of titles, none of which Jesus explicitly rejects, climaxing with the title Jesus is made to use for himself, "Son of Man."

Good novels will sometimes have the key to the plot concealed (and sometimes not so concealed) within the first chapter. John has done the same thing with his story. All that we read from John 2 on deals, sometimes subtly and implicitly and at other times directly and explicitly, with the issue of Jesus' identity.

One final feature of this section needs to be highlighted. Nathanael, in spite of all of his suspicion, believes in Jesus apparently on the basis of Jesus' marvelous words that he had seen Nathanael under the tree. Nathanael's belief seems incredible even to Jesus who then raises the question of the basis of belief. There are extraordinary experiences awaiting the disciples, Jesus says, but the most important is that the disciples will witness the intimate relationship between Jesus in this world and the divine realm far beyond this world (1:51).

PART ONE:
JESUS REVEALS GLORY
2:1—12:50

1

Signs and Speeches

2:1—5:47

Most students of the Fourth Gospel find a major division in the Gospel at the point of chapter 13. It is generally accepted that John 1—12 constitutes one unit of the document and John 12—21 another. In the first of these, the theme heard most frequently is that of Jesus' revelation of glory, that is, by act and word Jesus demonstrates the presence of God, confronting and challenging those who encounter him. Throughout this section, however, he again and again denies that his "hour" has come (for example, 2:4), while in 12:23 he asserts that the "hour" for his "glorification" has come. Hence, chapters 2—12 seem to focus on Jesus' public ministry and the expression of the divine presence in his life. Chapters 13—20, on the other hand, are the account of God's glorification of Jesus. The two parts may be thought of as horizontal and vertical lines intersecting one another. In the first part the primary movement is horizontal with Jesus offering the revelation of the Father to those whose lives he touches, while in the second part the Father bestows his honor on his own unique Son, the action being the vertical movement from God above to the Son here on earth. In the simplest of terms, it is possible to say that in the first twelve chapters Jesus *reveals* glory, while in the last eight Jesus *receives* glory.

That revealing of God's presence is what strikes us as we move from the historical beginnings of 1:19–51 into chapter 2. Through signs and speeches Jesus confronts humans with his identity which we have come at least vaguely to understand in chapter 1. In chapters 2—5 John's story unfolds in combinations of the acts of Jesus accompanied by his words. Now John is showing us what he meant in 1:14 when he claimed that the Christ-Word had become human, moving and living among us and revealing through his human life the glory of God. John will also pick up the relationship of Jesus to the Old Testament, introduced in 1:7–18, and the role of witness in the discovery of Jesus' identity, first brought forward in 1:6–8, 15, and 19–51.

THE FIRST OF THE SIGNS (2:1–11)

In 1:48–49 Nathanael was brought to an initial belief in Jesus as a result of what appears to be Jesus' wondrous knowledge. John in this way introduces the question of how one is to come to recognize the divine quality of this single human life. Now in chapter 2, in what John calls the first of the "signs," he narrates the account of a wonder done by Jesus at a wedding in Cana of Galilee and how it enabled the disciples to believe in Jesus. It should be noted that John likes the word "sign" to describe the marvelous deeds of Jesus. His preference for this word is not accidental, for he clearly thinks that these acts are like road signs pointing us in the proper direction. The signs direct those who experience the wonder, either firsthand or through John's retelling of it, toward Jesus himself. John will later state some reservations he has about a faith in Jesus that arises only from such signs, but here it is enough for us to understand that the wondrous act of Jesus is part of what John means by the revelation of glory in Jesus' life—the expression of Jesus' true identity.

The wedding scene is sketched ever so briefly, for John is not really interested in the wedding itself, but in the act of Jesus by which the depleted wine supply is replenished. The mundane human crisis is brought to the attention of Jesus by his mother. Jesus' mother (never mentioned by name in John's Gospel) would like to spare the hosts the embarrassment of running out of wine. She seems to suppose that Jesus could do something about the situation (perhaps this is the barest beginning of faith), but John does not hint at why she should think so. She is rebuked by her son in words that mean that Jesus will not be manipulated by any human. In his sovereignty he alone decides when and how his glory will be expressed. But the wine, nonetheless, is found where once there had been only water. Not incidentally the water was present for the purpose of Jewish religious practices of cleansing.

It is the result of the action that interests John, and 2:11 summarizes that interest: The SIGN expresses GLORY which evokes FAITH. It is in this case only the disciples who perceive the action of Jesus in such a way that they come to believe in him. This is not yet a sign intended for public consumption, but nonetheless the pattern is established. Through the actions of Jesus one can discern the presence of God in this man Jesus.

The act of changing water into wine is of interest to John because it has a symbolism beyond the simple wondrous act itself. The wonders of Jesus narrated by John are often exploited by the evangelist for their symbolic meaning, as we will learn in the course of seeing how he weaves them into his Jesus story. The marvelous production of wine from water suggests to John that Jesus' life and ministry are the re-creation of the Jewish faith. The point John wants to make is hinted at in the function the water jars had. They were used for the purification rites of the Jewish people (2:6). With the advent of Jesus the Hebraic-Jewish tradition is transformed from "water" into "wine." This is part of one of John's special themes, namely, that the revelation of God in Christ is the further and full maturation of the ancient tradition of God's work among the people of Israel.

John has hoisted another flag for us in this little narrative. Jesus' reply to his mother includes the words, "My hour has not yet come" (2:4). John already wants us to know that his narrative will move us steadily toward one great climax in which the "hour" does occur— the glorification of Jesus accomplished in the cross. This event he describes in the words of Jesus simply as the "hour." Here and throughout the chapters leading up to the passion narrative Jesus will reveal God's glory in his words and actions, but the "hour" of his life that will decisively bare his true identity is yet to come.

THE OLD TEMPLE AND THE NEW (2:12–25)

Jesus represents the final act in the drama of God's relationship with the people of Israel. John now tells us this in a narrative that has been traditionally called the "cleansing of the temple." Jesus and his followers go to Jerusalem for the Passover, and there he enters the temple and drives out those ever-present commercializers—those who are always there to make a quick buck in every situation. The narrative follows the basic form as we find it in the other Gospels but with two revealing differences. First, the place of the cleansing of the temple in the story of Jesus. For John this incident functions as the first public act of Jesus. The narrative is found here because John believes it is the paradigm of the whole of Jesus' life and ministry. Jesus' life means that Judaism—indeed human religion in general— can never be the same.

But the second thing that is significant for John is the discussion that follows the act of driving the commercializers out of the temple. The discussion that ensues (2:18–25) properly centers in the question "Who does Jesus think he is to presume to correct the practices of the temple personnel?" That is precisely what John wants his readers to begin to ask—who is this man anyway? The religious leaders ask Jesus to produce a "sign" that will satisfy them that he has authority to act in this way, but the sign Jesus mentions in response is misunderstood. When he says that he could rebuild the temple in three days after it is torn down, he is speaking of his own body. Jesus' authority is challenged, and his response is a reference to his own death and resurrection.

The temple is the dwelling place of God on earth. It is the point in space where one can find God among his people. But John claims that with Jesus the point in space has been shifted from the physical temple in Jerusalem to the person of Jesus himself. Only the resurrection will make that clear, but John signals the message already in this passage.

Jesus' presence in Jerusalem occasions a number of "signs," we are told in John 2:23. But the faith that these signs produce is immature and unreliable, and Jesus cannot trust himself to such superficial believers.

A LEARNED LEADER MEETS JESUS (3:1–21)

The way in which the revelation of God's glory challenges and transforms the established religion has been the focus of the sign at Cana and the temple narrative. It is this same theme that lurks in the shadows of the conversation between Jesus and Nicodemus. Nico-

demus characterizes for John the religious leader who senses correctly that Jesus offers a significant truth as one sent from God (3:2).
But Nicodemus cannot quite bring himself to believe in Jesus. Later
John will have Nicodemus speak out on behalf of Jesus (7:50–51) and
assist in the burial of Jesus (19:39). But here Nicodemus struggles in
vain to comprehend and embrace the revelation of God in Christ.

Nicodemus comes to Jesus under the cover of darkness which is
symbolic for John. Nicodemus's home is in the darkness of this
world, that is, its pervasive alienation from God. So the discussion
with this learned teacher is set within the contrast of the darkness of
the world (and the established religion) and the light of the world
found in Jesus. Indeed this passage is a commentary in part on
1:5—the darkness cannot comprehend the light. Nicodemus initiates
the conversation, but it is clear that Jesus is the one who controls the
subject of the discussion. Jesus insists that one must be "born again"
or "born from above"—the Greek word means both "again" and
"from above." This is to say that there must be a spiritual rebirth in
humans that is occasioned by the power of God present in the Spirit.
This Spirit freely moves among us as the wind, entirely free of human
control. (The word *pneuma* means both wind and spirit, and hence
allows the word play and tiny analogy of 3:8.) Nicodemus cannot
understand all of this, as 3:4 and 9 indicate. His misunderstanding,
however, simply occasions Jesus' further description of the subject.
John's way of handling conversations between Jesus and others often
follows this pattern: Jesus speaks, the listener(s) misunderstands him
and Jesus continues further to develop the theme. Moreover, as in
this case, Jesus is always in control of the conversation and determines its direction. John never allows Jesus to be anything but the
sovereign Lord in relationships with humans.

The dialogical nature of this incident is lost soon after 3:9, and the
conversation becomes a speech in which we are not sure whether
John wants us to think that Jesus is speaking, or the evangelist. The
plural pronouns in 3:11 suggest that it is the Christian community that
expresses its faith here. The speech moves on to an assertion of the
revelation of God in Christ (only the Son who comes from the divine
realm can reveal that realm to humans) and then to a metaphorical
reference to the crucifixion. Using the story of Moses and the bronze
serpent of Numbers 21, John quickly introduces us to the meaning he

will find in the crucifixion. "Lifting up" is what is done when a king is enthroned, but it is also what is done in the act of crucifying a criminal. So, Jesus' death will assuredly be a crucifixion—the most lowly and terrible kind of execution—but it will at the same time be the enthronement of the King of all creation.

The purpose of all of this—the sending of the Son into the world of sin and his death—is that humans might have a certain kind of life for which John's favorite description is "eternal life." It means simply the human life lived out of the context of a conscious relationship with God made possible through Christ. The divine effort in Christ is not for the purpose of judgment but for the salvation that is characterized as "eternal life." Judgment does occur, however, as a natural consequence of the presence of the divine will among humans. Some are proven to be evil by nature and others basically good by their response to Jesus. We will later hear more of John's concept of judgment, namely, that a person judges him- or herself by his or her response to Christ.

The flow of these ideas in 3:3–21 is hardly logical by our standards of logic. The movement from one idea to another in the discourses of the Fourth Gospel is most often not a "straight line development"; more characteristic of the movement of thought we find in Jesus' speeches in this Gospel is a "spiral" (or sometimes "elliptical") development. The figure on p. 28 should help the reader see the way in which the logic of the Nicodemus speech flows and prepare us for the longer discourses in the Gospel.

John has stated the way in which God's glory in the person of Jesus must affect the religious understanding of people in three forceful sections: the sign at Cana, the temple incident, and now the discussion with Nicodemus. John's broadside blasts at Judaism suggest to us that the relationship of Christianity and Judaism was one of his major concerns. That fact will be conveyed later on in even more pointed narratives and speeches.

THE BEST MAN HONORS THE GROOM (3:22–36)

Not unlike those interludes in the prologue that deal with John the Baptizer, this passage seems to be an aside, an excursus of sorts. Here again the concern seems to be the relationship of the Baptizer

THE "SPIRALING" CHARACTER OF THE
NICODEMUS DISCOURSE

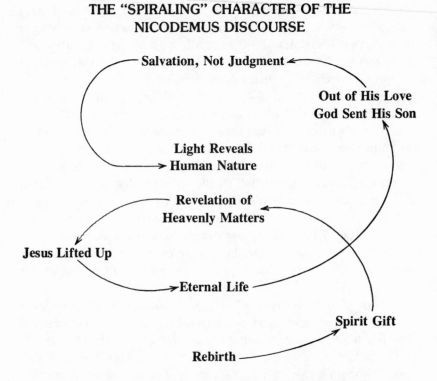

and Jesus. The section has three parts. The first (3:22–26) is a simple but believable setting for the words of the Baptizer. He and Jesus (or Jesus' disciples, depending on how one regards 4:2) are both baptizing, but Jesus appears to be attracting more attention, which naturally worries the disciples of the Baptizer. Hence they bring the matter to their master with understandable exaggeration: "EVERYONE is going to Jesus instead of to us!"

The second part of the little story (3:27–30) is comprised of the Baptizer's witness. You can give to others only what God has first given to you. The implication is that the Baptizer can do no more than witness to the one to whom God has given so much. The Baptizer compares himself with the best man at a wedding, whose purpose is not to be the center of attention but rather to stand beside and honor the groom. Consequently, Jesus must increase in prominence, while the Baptizer's role is to diminish.

To this simple little account of the witness of the Baptizer is

appended a minisermon which would appear not to be a continuation
of the Baptizer's words but the words of the evangelist occasioned by
the witness he puts on the lips of the Baptizer. Indeed, the words
sound like those of our evangelist. They begin with an important
theme in John's Gospel—the origin of Jesus. Since Jesus' origin is in
the divine realm, he is greater than all humans (and that statement
alone is the only clear link 3:31–36 has with the words of the Baptizer). Even though Jesus is not accepted, his words are God's words,
since God has filled him with the divine Spirit. The Father loves the
Son and that is the reason Jesus has God's power. Those who believe
in Jesus have eternal life, but those who are disobedient have no life
but only God's wrath. A decisive statement made in 3:36 is worth a
brief pause. Notice that the opposite of belief (v. 36) is disobedience.
The implication is that obedience in John's view is the willingness to
accept and trust, that is, to believe, Jesus. Obedience and disobedience are not matters of moral behavior as much as personal trust.

THE STORY OF SAMARITAN FAITH (4:1–42)

With the mention of belief and unbelief in 3:36 the evangelist finds a
natural transition to his next story, which is the tale of the faith of first
one Samaritan woman and then of an entire Samaritan village. But to
set the stage for Jesus' trip through Samaria the evangelist signals the
role Jerusalem and the whole of Judea are about to play in the Gospel.
When the Pharisees learn of Jesus' mounting success, there is some
talk (just what we are not told). Jesus then decides to leave the area
and return to Galilee. The role of rejection and danger has now been
attached to the region of Jerusalem and that role will be enhanced as
John develops his story. (Notice that 4:2 seems to be the effort of the
writer to correct what might have been a false inference of 3:22).

Jesus is passing through Samaria when he engages a woman at the
well in conversation. We might say that Jesus and this woman, at least
at first, have a communication problem, for here the evangelist em-
ploys his technique of having the listener misunderstand Jesus. Note
the following attempt to chart the strange course of this conversation:

4:7   Jesus requests a drink of water. (A *tangible* matter, water.)
4:8   The woman responds in surprise that a Jewish man would
      speak to her, a Samaritan woman.

4:10 Jesus then speaks of spiritual refreshment, living water. (An *intangible* matter.)

4:11 The woman understands Jesus to be speaking of water from the well and wonders how he intends to get the water without a bucket, for the well is very deep. (A concern for *tangible* matters.)

4:13 Jesus again speaks of a spiritual water that quenches one's spiritual longings once and for all. (An *intangible* subject.)

4:15 The Samaritan woman responds eagerly, "Quickly let me have that water, so that I won't have to carry water every day from this well!" (A *tangible* interest.)

John obviously believes that humans tend to misunderstand God's gift of salvation even when it stands before their very eyes. Like the Samaritan woman, humans are inclined to confuse the two realities of our physical and spiritual needs.

Jesus changes the conversation, and with his knowledge of the life situation of the woman wins her admiration. ("Sir, I perceive that you are a prophet" [4:19].) However, now it is she who changes the subject—the Jews and Samaritans have different ways and forms of worship. That matters not at all to Jesus who points out that worship is to be done in the Spirit and the Truth given to humans by the revelation of God in Christ. And that gift of the Spirit and that revelation of the Truth is *now*. The woman then hints at her growing faith by speaking of the Messiah, and Jesus answers her directly. His words are difficult to translate for they are the sober proclamation "I AM." These words are one of the ways in which John demonstrates Jesus' divine authority and truth. At any rate, Jesus declares himself to be the Messiah of whom the woman speaks.

The return of the disciples and their shock at finding Jesus talking with a woman—a Samaritan woman at that—allows the woman to slip off to her home and announce to the entire village, "Come, see a man who told me ALL that I ever did. Can this be the Messiah?" A nice touch of joyful exaggeration! The result is that the villagers come out to encounter Jesus, and they come to believe that Jesus is the "Savior of the world" (4:42)—the only time John uses that title for Jesus. Their faith is no longer secondhand, dependent on the witness of the woman, but firsthand. Furthermore, their faith exceeds that of the one who pointed them to Christ to begin with (v. 42). A fitting climax to the story.

John uses this little tale of the Samaritan woman to make a number of points, it would appear. One is clearly stated in the discussion with the disciples inserted into the story which has its primary focus on the Samaritans and their faith. In that conversation (4:31–38) Jesus points the disciples to the rich possibilities of faith among the Samaritans. John 4:37 suggests that one may not always experience the results of efforts to lead others to faith, even though one's successors will. But notice the context within which John has set this story. We have been shown that Judaism will be transformed by the revelation of God in Christ, and we have encountered a wise teacher of the Law who cannot understand Jesus. The Baptizer's witness only seems to stir the hostile concerns of the religious leaders (4:1). But now we are confronted with an account of the amazing readiness to believe among those despised half-breeds, the Samaritans. John surely implies by the positioning of these narratives of chapters 3 and 4 a contrast between Nicodemus and the Samaritan woman. The religious establishment will fail to embrace the truth of God, even though the heretical Samaritans do!

Still another theme in this story is important to mention. John has again brought our attention to the importance of witness. The Baptizer's witness has been mentioned, but now a woman whose own faith is immature and uncertain (note the tentative nature of her proclamation in 4:29) points others to Christ, and they come to a faith more profound and solid than the faith of the witness. In summary, John has demonstrated the way in which the revelation of God is offered to those who stand outside of the fold of the religious establishment and the way in which the despised heretics of the day see more clearly than do the learned doctors of the established religion.

THE FAITH OF A ROYAL OFFICIAL:
SECOND SIGN (4:43–54)

These two stories of faith—the Samaritans and now the royal official—are linked together in several ways, not the least of which is the fact that they are both stories of the faith of persons outside of or on the fringes of the established religion of the day. The royal official in this story was probably a servant of King Herod, and as such was considered to be on the margins of the Jewish faith, at least in the view of the religious leaders. But these two stories are also both expressions of a believing response to Jesus and as such serve our evangelist's purpose of exploring the meaning of authentic faith.

The account of the healing of the son of the royal official is introduced with a paragraph that raises questions for the careful reader (4:43–45). We are told that Jesus returns to Galilee after two days in Samaria. 4:45 reports that the Galileans welcomed Jesus because of all that he had done in Jerusalem. We are given the impression that the Galileans are far more receptive of Jesus than were the people of Jerusalem, and it appears (as we mentioned above) that Galilee is gradually emerging as the region of faith in contrast to Jerusalem, the region of rejection. However, 4:44 suggests something quite different. Either it is a contradiction of 4:45, or else we are to look for a subtle way in which Jesus experiences rejection in Galilee, in spite of the apparent faith of the people there. 4:44 seems hardly to fit the context of this short paragraph. The way in which it does fit the entire story (4:43–54) is evident when we consider the theme of the healing about to take place. In this healing story we find a rebuke of the tendency of persons to believe in Jesus solely on the grounds of the wondrous nature of his works (v. 48). As a matter of fact, 4:45 indicates that this is *precisely* the reason the Galileans welcome Jesus—because they had seen all that he had done in Jerusalem. The subtle implication of 4:44 prepares us for the discussion of faith and signs about to be narrated in 4:46–53.

The setting is again Cana where Jesus had done his first sign (2:1–11). The royal official hears of Jesus' return to the region and goes to him in order to plead with Jesus to come to his home in Capernaum and heal his dying son. Jesus' response seems harsh and unnecessary: "If you do not see signs and wonders, you will not believe." The official will not, however, be discouraged, and he pleads again for Jesus' help. Jesus then declares that he can go home, for his son will live. The official believes the declaration and returns to his home to find that his son recovered at the very time Jesus promised it would be so. He and his entire house believe. The evangelist concludes the story by reminding us that this is the second sign Jesus had done in Galilee.

The function of this story is hardly obscure. In John's plan for this section of his Gospel it takes up the idea that the signs evoke faith from those who experience them. But it is also a story that raises serious questions about the role of signs in relationship to true faith in Jesus. The evangelist here begins to distinguish between two ways in which the signs of Jesus may be perceived. Jesus' rebuke in 4:48 implies that an attraction to Jesus on the basis of his marvelous acts alone is not a mature (or shall we say authentic) faith. Not yet clear, but perhaps implied, is the fact that seeing *through* the sign beyond the wondrous features to the identity of the performer is the true and authentic way of perceiving signs. It appears that the official's faith is indeed deeper than an awesome attraction to this one who does wonders. His persistent belief that Jesus can help him (v. 49) is John's way of saying that this man is not simply a "signs-believer." His faith is genuine!

A further note at this point is important. The signs of Jesus in the Gospel of John are few in number but mightily impressive. We will see that in each case the wonder attributed to Jesus is extreme. In this case, it is a healing done at a distance—Jesus is not even in the presence of the little boy whom he heals!

AUTHORITY AND WITNESS:
THIRD SIGN (5:1–47)

There are at least four units of material in John 5, but it is difficult to cut the chapter into independent parts, since John has woven them together rather tightly. There is first a story of a healing (5:1–9), then a discussion of the violation of the Sabbath done in the healing (5:10–18), followed by a discourse on the relationship of the Father and the Son (5:19–29), and finally the conclusion—the witnesses to Jesus (5:30–47).

The healing of the man at the pool is told with John's typical and amazing brevity. First, Jesus returns to Jerusalem for a feast—which feast it was, we are not told. (Most likely the reference is to the Feast of "Weeks" or Pentecost.) Then, we are given a careful description of the setting for the healing (5:2–4). Finally in no more than four verses the healing itself is told. It has just been suggested that the signs of Jesus in the Fourth Gospel are invariably acts of extreme wonder. In this case, the man is entirely hopeless. Plagued with his illness now for thirty-eight years, he is unable to move quickly enough into the pool to avail himself of its healing waters. As hopeless as his situation is, so quickly and simply does the Johannine Jesus effect the healing! All that Jesus requires of the lame man is a statement that he wants to be well. The man answers Jesus by pointing out the hopelessness of his situation. Jesus then simply orders him to get up and walk away with his mat under his arm. As simple as that, healing is done!

John is not nearly so interested in the healing as he is in the discussion that follows the healing. Here is another incident in which John narrates a sign, but then spends most of his time in the discussion of the symbolic meaning of the sign. In this case, it is Jesus' authority over the Sabbath regulations that figures most prominently in the discussion. 5:9b–18 sets up the conflict between Jesus and the religious leaders on the question of the Sabbath. The man has been instructed to violate the Sabbath by the act of carrying his bed. The religious leaders (whom John calls simply "the Jews") want to know who had instructed the man to carry his bed, but he does not know the name of the one who healed him after all those years. When he encounters Jesus later in the temple, he quickly identifies him, so that the religious leaders can charge Jesus with the violation of the Sabbath. In contrast to the faith of the official after the healing of his son (4:43), there is no evidence of faith on the part of this fellow. Rather, he even goes so far as to "rat" on Jesus to the religious leaders. The sign can evoke faith, as it does in the case of the royal official, but it can also fail to evoke faith, as it does in this case. Jesus' words to the man when they meet again in the temple may be suggestive of the dim view John takes of this failure to see through the sign to the sign-doer. Jesus says, "See, you are well! Sin no more, that nothing worse befall you" (5:14). Given John's concern in this story, it is not necessary to take these words as an endorsement of the relationship between sin and human affliction. John more than likely has Jesus speaking about the spiritual condition of this man who has at last been made well physically. He must now concern himself with the matter of his relationship with God (and hence with Jesus); it is in this sphere of holistic health that the man is still in need.

Thanks to this dimwitted and ungrateful fellow who points Jesus out to the religious leaders, Jesus in now engaged in the debate over the meaning of the Sabbath law. Jesus' defense is that since his Father works on the Sabbath and every day to heal humanity, so Jesus' work stands above the Sabbath regulations. He has claimed for himself an authority that transcends that of Moses and the Law. The religious leaders do not like this, and charge him with both the violation of the Sabbath and with making himself God's equal. This may be another incident of Johannine misunderstanding, because Jesus has not really claimed equality with God in what he is reported to have said. Yet ironically his opponents state the real truth that John is helping us see, namely, Jesus' relationship with God.

The stage is set now for the third act in the drama of John 5. In this case, the act is comprised entirely of a soliloquy. Jesus' defense of his working on the Sabbath gives occasion for a lengthy statement about the relationship of the Father and the Son. The affirmations of this discourse in summary are these: (1) the Son does not act on his own; he imitates the Father (5:19); (2) the Father loves the Son (5:20); (3) the Father reveals himself to the Son (5:20); (4) the Father gives the Son authority over resurrection (5:21) and judgment (5:22); and (5) the human response to Jesus is, therefore, a response to the Father (5:23).

The content of 5:19–23 leads to the discussion of the authority of the Son over matters that concern the "last days"—the crucial matters of life, death, resurrection, and judgment. The thrust of these verses is to articulate the *functional unity* of the Father and the Son, that is to say, the Son functions for the Father and with equal authority. 5:24–29 affirms this functional unity with regard to the crucial matters of the "last days" in two different ways. First, the Son functions for the Father in terms of those features of the last day that are already present in Jesus: (1) one who believes in the Father, through the Son whom the Father sent, already *has* eternal life (5:24a); (2) such a person has passed beyond judgment and death (5:24b); (3) now in Jesus' presence the resurrection ("coming to life") is already a reality, because the Son is the source of life on behalf of the Father (5:26); and (4) the Son has the power of judgment now in this life (5:27).

Second, the Son functions for the Father in terms of those features of the last day that are yet to come: (1) the dead will hear the voice of the Son (5:28); and (2) they will come out of their tombs and will be judged (5:29).

The drift of all of this is that the Son functions for the Father in this world at this time and at the end of time and in the next world. From the simpler assertion of the Son's authority to command the violation of the Sabbath we have come directly into the heart of John's view of Jesus. The path of this chapter thus looks like this (so far):

A healing ------>Sabbath laws ----->The Son's unity
with the Father.

The last link in this chain of thoughts is the question of the witnesses to Jesus' authority. That is, who demonstrates by their words and actions that this relationship between the Father and the Son just described is indeed the case?

In 5:31–47 Jesus begins by acknowledging that his own witness to himself is not enough; it is not valid by legal procedures. More than one witness is needed to sustain a case (see Deut. 19:15). But then Jesus lists four different witnesses. The first is a man—*John, the Baptizer*. The second is comprised of the *works that Jesus himself does*. Since those works are given to Jesus to do by the Father, the *Father* is a vocal witness on behalf of Jesus. That they reject Jesus is evidence that they do not hear the words of the Father. But they do read the *scriptures*, and these are the fourth witness to the truth of Jesus' claims. All of these point toward the truth of what Jesus claims for himself.

John 5:41–47 serves as a summary conclusion of the chapter with its four interrelated subunits. The rejection of Jesus convicts the people of their own blindness and lack of love of God. They are so misguided that they will accept one who comes with only his or her own authority, while they will not accept one who comes with God's authority. The closing blow is a mighty one that strikes a sensitive spot in the lives of the religious leaders. Moses, their ancestor and guide, will convict them. Moses witnesses to Jesus (the witness of Scripture, v. 39) for it is of Jesus that Moses writes. Therefore the religious leaders are judged on the basis of their *own* criterion and convicted by it. The reason they cannot believe Jesus is that they do not *really believe* Moses and his words.

And with this last point we are brought back to the beginning of the whole unit, 2:1—5:47, in which we find that Christ causes a transformation of the Jewish faith (the Cana sign and the temple incident). In fact we are driven back to the cosmic beginning of John's story of Jesus. He is rejected by his own people (1:11) even though he is the completion and fulfillment of the religious faith by which they intend to structure their lives (1:17–18).

SIGNS AND SPEECHES—AN OVERVIEW
(2:1—5:47)

THEME ONE	THEME TWO

Christ's truth transforms and fulfills the Hebraic-Jewish tradition

The witnesses to Christ's truth

The Cana Sign
(2:1–11)

Christ is the "new wine" produced out of the water of the Hebraic-Jewish tradition.

The sign of changing water into wine witnesses to Christ and evokes faith.

The Cleansing and Replacement of the Temple (2:12–25)

The Nicodemus Discourse (3:1–21)
A radical new rebirth is required.

John, the Baptizer, honors and points to Jesus (3:22–36)

Samaritan Faith (4:1–42)

The faith of the Samaritans contrasts with the failure of Nicodemus to understand Jesus.

The witness of the Samaritan woman epitomizes the role of witness.

The Sign of the Healing of the Royal Official's Son (4:43–54)

The Healing of the Man with the Thirty-Eight-Year Illness and Resulting Discourse (5:1–47)

Christ's authority over the Sabbath regulations and the conviction of the religious leaders.

The witnesses to Jesus.

SUMMARY

It appears clear that John 2—5 hammers away at two essential themes—the transformation of the Hebraic-Jewish tradition, resulting from the revelation of God in Christ, and the role of witnesses to Christ. (See the chart above.) What we have before us is a trial scene in which the defense is arguing that Jesus is not a traitor to the Jewish faith and the Hebraic tradition, but actually one who completes the meaning of that faith and tradition. But, like one of the signs of Jesus, all of this points beyond itself to additional themes to be fleshed out in greater detail. The signs and speeches of John 2—5 only whet our appetites for more. And John intends to satisfy our need, in part at least, with food of both the earthly and the heavenly variety.

2
Food, Earthly and Heavenly

6:1–71

John 6 functions as the hinge upon which the first half of the Gospel pivots. It is the fulcrum upon which the heavy weight of division and opposition begins to tilt the drama. It is in the course of this chapter that opposition leaps up in threatening proportions to begin to take its awesome role in the story. It is really a relatively simple chapter. First, there is the sign of the feeding of the multitude followed by the two-in-one sign of the walking on the water and the miraculous landing. These signs lead to a lengthy discourse with several parts which is concluded with the sober words regarding faltering faith and explicit unbelief.

EARTHLY FOOD AND WONDERS ON THE SEA: FOURTH AND FIFTH SIGNS (6:1–21)

The feeding of the multitude, we are told, takes place in Galilee, even though the events of chapter 5 seem to be set in Jerusalem (5:1), and there is no announcement of Jesus' return to Galilee. It might seem that chapter 4 would more naturally precede chapter 6. But perhaps John's concern is less with geography than theology, and it is understandable that these signs and the discussion that ensues from them should take place in Galilee where Jesus' signs have been eagerly welcomed, if not always understood. The Galileans are now confronted with their nearsightedness.

The feeding of the multitude is simply narrated, as is John's custom. We are told (not without significance) that the Passover feast was rapidly approaching (6:4). Jesus raises the question of feeding the crowd that had gathered about him, but John reminds us that Jesus knew exactly what he would do. The five loaves of barley bread and two tiny fish are discovered—the lunch of a boy who had joined the crowd. Those meager morsels wondrously feed the entire crowd (five thousand men alone, John tells us [6:10]), and it takes twelve baskets to gather the leftovers. The people understandably declare that this Jesus must be the long-awaited prophet, one like Moses, who was expected by some to be God's anointed. Jesus wants none of their efforts to impose a royal office on him, and he retreats to the hills.

The two-in-one sign (6:16–21) begins with the disciples going back across the lake, while Jesus remains on the other side alone. In the midst of a brewing storm the disciples see Jesus walking toward them on the water. The scene is clearly one of theophany—the revelation of the presence of God—and the disciples are rightly terrified. Jesus' response underscores the fact that this is a revelatory act: "I AM," he says to them (v. 20). They take him into the boat, and suddenly find themselves on the shore—the second wondrous event of this one narrative. John's employment of the wondrous revelation of God on the water is characteristic of some of his other narratives. It is simply told but with an emphasis on the divine authority of the figure of Jesus. The chaotic waters threaten the existence of his followers, and they are in danger of being pulled into the chaos. But a simple "I AM" from Jesus saves them and brings them safely to the shore.

The positioning of the walking on water and miraculous landing narrative between the feeding of the multitude and the discourse on the bread of life suggests a kind of "related fact" that John wants in the picture before launching into the discourse. In one way, the movement directly from the feeding story into the discourse would be smoother and more logical. We think that until we realize John wants his readers to know that Christ is indeed one who stands as Lord over the forces of chaos and that even the natural world responds to his presence. Upon reflection one can see another theme implicitly arising out of these stories of wondrous acts. There is a haunting sense in which the stories entice the mind back to another figure and another time, the feeding of the children of Israel in the desert under the leadership of Moses. It is for that reason John dates the feeding near the time of Passover (6:4). Certainly the "murmurings" of the crowd later on in the discourse (6:41, 60) recall the murmurings of the people of Israel against Moses as they wandered in the desert (Exodus 16). Could the stilling of the waters and the miraculous landing be intended to arouse memories of that wondrous escape from Egypt by the people of Israel? The chaotic waters came under the control of Moses, and the people miraculously crossed over to the other shore of the Sea of Reeds. The subtle tones of the Exodus experience combine here with the awe inspired by the two-in-one sign. With those tones John provides the reader with a background upon which he or she can now paint a provocative foreground—Jesus in his flesh-and-blood reality is the bread of life, the manna from heaven.

THE BREAD OF LIFE— HEAVENLY FOOD (6:22-71)

The word is out! This fellow Jesus serves free meals! And so the crowd swells and seeks this wandering "free-groceries man." The brief narrative introduces the conversation that takes place in 6:25 and following. The crowd seeks Jesus for all the wrong reasons, and John makes their absence of faith stand out more vividly in the first question they ask of Jesus: "When did you get here?" Their question has only a geographical/temporal concern but ironically expresses their theological blindness. They know nothing of the real question of when the revealer of God appeared in this world.

The conversation is similar to the one found in John 3 between Jesus and Nicodemus. Jesus' concerns seem to go right over the heads of the more literal and materialistically minded crowd. Jesus confronts them with the fact that they are here to see him because they want another free meal and not because they "saw signs" (6:26). In apparent contrast with 4:48, "seeing signs" here seems to mean a perception of Jesus' identity behind the actual wonder itself. The crowd, however, is interested only in the marvel itself and how that marvel benefits them, not a discernment in faith of the one responsible for the marvel. Jesus advises the crowd that they should attend to a food that remains (one of John's favorite words, *menein*) to eternal life, and it is this food Jesus has to offer them (6:27). Their response seems to be an unrelated question, "What can we do to the works of God?" There is only one work that is needed, replies Jesus—belief in the one sent by God (6:29). Now the people want a sign from Jesus so that they are able to believe in him. They want manna from heaven similar to the kind Moses provided for the people of Israel. Jesus then breaks the cycle of questions to move to the heart of the issue: Jesus is the true bread from heaven—the bread that satisfies hunger once and for all (6:32–33). (We are reminded of the similar statement made of the "living water" to the woman at the well in 4:14.)

John 6:36–40 constitutes the first discourse link of the section. The cycle of themes here runs as follows: belief in Jesus, who is sent from the Father to do his will, which is preserving those who believe for eternal life. At 6:41 we have the first instance of misunderstanding; and it is expressed in terms of the "murmuring" of the people. What they are puzzled over is the fact that this fellow is the son of Joseph, so how can he say that he has come down from heaven? Through the author's use of irony he has again raised the theological question of the identity of Jesus by means of the question of Jesus' origin. The inability of the crowd to discern the truth—that Jesus is indeed the bread that originates in the divine realm and is graciously offered to them—arises from their familiarity with the earthly origin of Jesus. Again the crowd is portrayed as bogged down in the literal, the superficial, and materialistic reality.

John 6:43–51 makes up the next segment of discourse, and in Johannine style it spirals through some of the same themes introduced in 6:36–40 but moves beyond them to additional matters. Only the one sent from God has seen God; and he (Jesus) is the bread of life—the living bread—which comes down from heaven and is superior to the manna eaten in the desert by Israel, because living bread results in eternal life for those who eat it. Jesus has claimed that he is the bread from heaven, the living bread; but in 6:51 John has him make this claim in an exaggerated way: The one who "devours" his flesh lives forever.

There follows another misunderstanding. The crowd cannot understand how it is that Jesus could give his flesh to be eaten (6:52). Now the statement is even more extreme: The one "gnawing" (or audibly munching) Jesus' flesh has eternal life and will be raised from the dead. This eating and drinking is the means by which one lives in

Jesus, and since Jesus lives that person will also live. Now the disciples (meaning here simply the believers) have had too much, and they cannot believe all of this (6:60).

Before coming to the grand climax of this complex discourse, perhaps we should look back and see what it is that John has accomplished through this section. Jesus makes a series of mounting claims for himself, each one becoming more radical than the previous. Punctuating these claims is the misunderstanding and murmuring of the crowd. The claims which stand out through this section and the corresponding scandalizing of the crowd are these:

—I am the bread of life (6:35).
   Murmuring—He is Joseph's son (6:41–42).
—The bread from heaven, which is superior to the manna
      given by Moses, is my flesh (6:49–51).
   Misunderstanding—How can he give his flesh to be
      eaten? (6:52).
—Those who gnaw on my flesh and drink my blood live in
      me (6:54–58).
   Murmuring—the disciples cannot accept this (6:60).

The more radically Jesus is made to express the central theme of the discourse, the more unbelieving becomes the crowd, until finally it is his own followers who cannot believe him. To them Jesus restates the essential theme in a still different way: "My words are Spirit, and it is Spirit which gives life. No one comes to me unless the Father gives him or her to me" (cf. 6:63–65). And again many of the disciples turn away. When Jesus challenges the remaining followers (now the "Twelve"), it is Peter who speaks for them. Finally, Jesus acknowledges the faith of the Twelve and predicts the betrayal of Judas (6:70–71).

SUMMARY

What a chapter this is! Here Jesus *acts* in such a way as to reveal his true identity as the one sent from the Father and as the one who does more than even the great Moses. Moreover, here Jesus *articulates* in ever more explicit and vivid word pictures that he is the one sent from the Father and in whom humans have the opportunity for lasting and meaningful life. Whatever the subtle meanings of the discourse materials, it is clear that John wants his readers to understand the full implications of God's act of revealing himself in a flesh-and-blood human being. Only by devouring this person Jesus—taking the full life of the revealer into yourself—can you grasp the gift of the revelation. Equally as clear as the act of revelation in this chapter is the reality of the rejection of the revelation. The correlative of revelation is unbelief! But for those who can believe, there is life. The message of much of this Gospel is the sober truth that humans lack even the basic instinct to recognize the truth of life when it stands before them.

Another observation merits repeating here: This whole treatment of the revealer and the rejection of him is framed within the borders of the history of the people of Israel. Not only do the dating of the incident "near the Passover" and the marvelous acts early in chapter 6 recall the experiences of the Exodus but also the discourse explicitly poses the gift of God in Christ in relationship to the manna God gave the children of Israel in the midst of their desert wanderings. Furthermore, just as the people of Israel murmur in discontent over Moses (for example, Num. 11:1), so the crowd and even the believers murmur in unbelief as they hear Jesus' claims for himself. John is emphasizing again the fact that the revelation of the Father in Christ transforms and fulfills the ancient Hebraic tradition. God in Christ has completed what was begun in his saving actions in the history of Israel, but the stubbornness of human refusal to believe is the same.

3

In Jerusalem

7:1—10:42

The mounting movement of unbelief and hostility toward Jesus is traced through the next six chapters in two phases: first in the conflict with the religious establishment in Jerusalem (7:1—10:42) and then in the final solidifying of the death plot against Jesus (11:1—12:50). The first phase opens on the sour note of unbelief and danger. 7:1–9 is a brief introduction to the ministry of Jesus in Jerusalem, which articulates the dangers awaiting Jesus in the capital city and the painful fact of the unbelief of Jesus' "brothers." While Jesus claims that this particular time is not the ripe time for him, he goes secretly to Jerusalem for the Feast of Tabernacles. In the context of that feast and presumably within the temple itself, Jesus addresses the crowds.

MEETING THE OPPONENTS ON THEIR OWN GROUND— DIVISION AND OPPOSITION (7:11–52)

Hearing him speak in the temple, people are amazed at Jesus' wisdom and raise the question of the source of his teachings. The discourse in 7:16–24 begins with the claim that Jesus' teachings are from God, and he seeks only the glory of God. But the crowd does not understand his statement that some are trying to kill him, and they declare that he is possessed by a demon. In 7:21–24 there is a defense of Jesus' act of healing done on a Sabbath (perhaps a reference back to 5:9, where Jesus' healing of the paralyzed man is done on the Sabbath). In the simplest of terms Jesus claims that his healing on the Sabbath is not a violation of the Sabbath laws.

A bit of Johannine irony appears here in the story. The people are amazed at Jesus' boldness in teaching in public. But they know that he is not the Messiah because, when the Messiah comes, no one will know from where he comes. They know where Jesus is from, therefore, Jesus is not the Messiah. The point is, of course, that they do *not* know where Jesus is from, but only his earthly roots (as is the case in 6:42). Jesus responds to this by declaring that people do not know his origin, but he does—it is from God. In 7:30–31 John suggests the ambivalence of the crowd—some try to arrest him but fail, since Jesus' "hour" has not come; and others believe in him, since his signs are so marvelous. Still another effort to arrest him seems unsuccessful and still another statement by Jesus evokes yet another misunderstanding. He speaks of his departure (his return to the Father), and the crowd wonders if he will go off to teach the Greeks living in the Roman Empire. Ironically, they are correct, of course. Jesus will eventually teach among the Greeks as Christianity is spread throughout the empire.

On another occasion in the temple, we are told, Jesus speaks again (7:37–39). It is the familiar theme of the living water that appears here. Jesus cites a passage of Scripture (which is not recognizable as a reference to any single passage in the Old Testament). The point is that the believer will be filled with the living water to the point of overflowing and that water is none other than the Spirit. (John here explains that the reference to the Spirit was not recognized until after Jesus' resurrection.)

We are now given two short scenes representative of the division and opposition. The crowd is divided among themselves as to the identity of Jesus (7:40–44). The religious leaders, however, are determined to put a halt to his teaching. The guards have been unsuccessful in arresting him, and now Nicodemus suggests that Jesus must be given a full hearing under the law. But the logic of the religious leaders is relentless: This man is from Galilee, and no prophet ever comes out of Galilee. Once again it is the theme of Jesus' origin that occasions misunderstanding and mistakenly sanctions unbelief (7:45–52).

This section is comprised of a series of short scenes which at first seem to wander aimlessly among three characters or groups of characters—Jesus, the crowd, and the religious leaders. But on closer examination one perceives the purpose of the evangelist through all of this. Beginning from the base of 7:1–9, which introduces the motifs of danger and unbelief, the evangelist has structured antiphonal speeches and acts. Jesus claims he comes from God, and the people respond that he is possessed by a demon. Jesus claims that his act of healing on the Sabbath does not violate the Sabbath laws, and there is ironic misunderstanding of his origin. Again, Jesus claims to come from the Father; the crowd answers back with division and the religious leaders answer with an effort to arrest Jesus. Jesus speaks of his return to the Father, and the response is again ironic misunderstanding of his destiny. He speaks of living waters, and the answer is division among both the people and the leaders. The final scene ends with another instance of misunderstanding centered on the issue of Jesus' origin. John has treated us here to still another dramatic portrayal of the inability of humans to grasp the origin and destiny of the revealer and the unyielding effort of the religious leaders to put an end to Jesus' teachings.

MEETING THE OPPONENTS ON THEIR OWN GROUND— ANCESTRY (8:12–59)

Now the theme of Jesus' identity, origin, and destiny are fleshed out for us. There are two cycles or dialogues in this section. An underlying motif is the question of ancestry—Jesus' and the people's. In the first cycle it is Jesus' identity and origin that stands front stage; in the second the ancestry of the crowds is the primary focus.

The first little cycle of dialogue (8:12–30) begins with one of the "I AM" sayings: "I am the light of the world." But we will hear more of that in the next chapter. The immediate concern is the witness to Jesus' identity. He is charged with testifying for himself, but he insists that his origin and destiny place him beyond the judgment of his critics. His ancestry is referred to not only here (v. 14) but again in 8:21, 23–24, and 28. The dramatic "I AM," with its solemn claim to divine authority, is also a statement of Jesus' ancestry, for it is an implicit claim to be from God (vv. 12, 24, 28). Jesus is not only from the Father but faithful to the Father (vv. 19, 26, 28, 29).

Dotted throughout these statements of Jesus' are the charges, questions, and bewilderment of the crowd. They charge that Jesus is testifying on his own behalf; they ask who his Father is and more simply, "Who are you?" They misunderstand his statement that he is going away where they cannot come to mean that he is going to kill himself. And finally they simply do not understand. Amazingly enough, however, we are told that many who heard him say these things believed in him.

The second cycle of dialogue (8:31–59) picks up on the note of belief on which the first cycle concludes but ends at the other extreme of the unbelief of the crowd. The spotlight in this cycle focuses on the ancestry of the crowd. Now the question is turned on them—who is your father? Jesus begins with the exploration of the freedom of those who are children of truth (vv. 31–36) and out of that grows his charge that the crowd is not Abraham's children at all, as they claim, but children of the devil (vv. 33–47). As the first dialogue began with the charge that Jesus is testifying for himself, this cycle concludes with his insistence that he does not seek his glory but only glory for the Father (vv. 49–58).

Through all of this the crowd's participation grows increasingly angry and defensive. They claim that Abraham is their Father (8:33, 39), but also that God is their Father (v. 41). Again they cry out that Jesus is possessed by a demon and (interestingly enough) is a Samaritan! (Perhaps just two ways of saying the same thing for the crowd.) Then finally they are incensed by the claim that Abraham saw Jesus' day and rejoiced in it. Their anger is increased by their misunderstanding of Jesus: "You are not fifty years old and yet you claim to have seen Abraham!" (v. 57). The second cycle ends with Jesus' boldest claim: "Before Abraham was I AM." At this the crowd gathers stones to kill him for his blasphemy (v. 59). What began on a positive note of belief ends in violent unbelief.

The question of ancestry is central because belief in Jesus necessitates understanding Jesus' ancestry (that is, he is from above, from the Father). If the crowd were truly children of Abraham, they would perceive the truth of Jesus' claims; but since they are in fact children of the devil, they find his claims incredible. For John the source of one's *orientation* (we might call it "roots") determines one's *perception*. John has brought us then from the discovery of the meaning of blindness to the revelation of God in Christ.

BLINDNESS—PHYSICAL AND SPIRITUAL: SIXTH SIGN (9:1–41)

"I am the light of the world" of 8:12 alerts the reader that the theme John here pursues is that of being able to perceive correctly the ancestry of Jesus. He now confronts us with this theme through an extended narrative. Chapter 9 is one of John's typical and favorite literary constructions. He will tell us a simple healing story, but then expand upon it until we see that the story is not only about the healing of physical blindness. It is a discussion of spiritual blindness. There are seven segments in the chapter. We call them scenes and treat chapter 9 as a minidrama.

The first scene is the healing story itself (9:1–7), but the actual healing is confined to vv. 6 and 7, and the previous five verses and introduction. That introduction involves Jesus' refusal to discuss the theological niceties of the situation of the man born blind. Then Jesus repeats his pronouncement of 8:12: "I am the light of the world." The healing itself is told with typical Johannine economy. The blind man's useless eyes are packed with mud, he is told to go and wash in the pool, he does so, and he can see! But the story has only begun!

The second scene (9:8–12) describes the reaction of the crowd. We are not surprised to hear that the crowd is divided in their assessment of the situation. The man who has just been healed is asked to tell the crowd about it, and in the simplest of terms he tells them about the acts and commands of "a man named Jesus." He has made the first of a series of witnesses.

The third scene (9:13–17) reports the first interrogation of the healed man by the religious authorities. They are brought into this matter because the healing has taken place on the Sabbath, and so they must determine whether or not the Sabbath regulations have been violated. (We are reminded of the healing in John 5 and what a contrast there is between the two beneficiaries of Jesus' healing acts—the lame man of chap. 5 and the blind man of chap. 9.) The healed man makes his second witness—again simple and straight-forward. The Pharisees are divided in their opinions on the matter, and so they ask the man what he thinks of the one who performed this healing. The man responds that Jesus is surely a "prophet."

The fourth scene (9:18–23) begins with the unbelief of the religious leaders. Interestingly it is the Pharisees who are said to be the inter-rogators in the third scene, and now it is simply "the Jews." This seems to indicate that for the evangelist the distinctions among the religious leaders were not important. They now call on the parents of the man. The parents are understandably frightened and are non-committal. "Ask him! He is an adult!"

In the fifth scene (9:24–34) we find the second interrogation of the healed man, and this time he is more aggressive. The minds of the leaders are made up; they only want the healed man to say what they want him to say. His witness is again simple: "I was blind and now I see. What else matters?" And he taunts them: "Do you want to become one of the followers of this healer?" This angers them, and they charge him with being a follower of Jesus, while they themselves are followers of Moses. (Once again it is a question of ancestry.) They cannot believe in Jesus for they do not know where he is from. The healed man points out the farcical nature of their position: Jesus has opened the man's eyes, and the leaders do not know where he is from. Surely, the man asserts, this Jesus is a "man from God"—how else could he do what he has done? (Another witness to this one who healed him.) The leaders throw him out for trying to teach them!

In scene six (9:35–38) there occurs the second meeting of the man and Jesus—their first encounter since the man's eyes have been opened. For some twenty-eight verses now Jesus has been "off-stage," and the action has been focused on the religious leaders, the healed man, and his parents. After a brief dialogue, the healed man makes his highest confession: "I believe, Lord."

Scene seven (9:39–41) concludes the drama. There is an ab-breviated exchange between Jesus and the religious leaders. In a declaration which is a digest of the whole narrative of chapter 9, Jesus says, "For judgment I came into this world, that those who do not see may see, and that those who see may become blind." In case the reader misses the point, John has the Pharisees ask (haughtily, we should imagine) if those words were aimed at them. Jesus has the last word: "If you were blind, you would have no guilt; but now that you say, 'We see,' your guilt remains." The point seems to be that the religious leaders claim that they know and see the truth, when in fact they are ignorant and blind. The truth of God's revelation only deepens their darkness because they refuse to see. Hence, their blindness is of their own making, and they are guilty as charged. Although they had been conducting the trial up to this point, it is they who are found guilty.

Chapter 9 has led us slowly to understand that the healing of the blind man's physical ailment is but the symbol of the healing of a spiritual blindness. It is intentional that the faith of the healed man has steadily grown from his first witness to his last confession. First, he says Jesus is a man (v. 11), then a prophet (v. 17), then a man from God (v. 33), and finally Lord (v. 38). At the same time as the healed man's faith is blossoming, increasingly with each segment, the religious leaders are falling further and further into the sightlessness of their unbelief. Jesus' strong condemnation of the blindness of the religious leaders is a frontal attack upon the religious establishment, which John will now continue to treat with a series of interrelated allegories.

SHEEP, SHEPHERDS, AND GATES (10:1–42)

As we enter into this first Johannine allegory, we may be tempted to put behind us the combat waged between Jesus and those who are blind to him. But actually the allegory we are about to consider is as powerful in what it condemns as it is in what it affirms. It is an allegory in the sense that several aspects of one reality (sheep, shepherds, hired workers, and gates to pasture) are used as metaphors to understand another reality (Jesus, believers, and leaders). In one way we might call this a parable, but it is quite different from the story parables we know from the other Gospels (for example, the Good Samaritan) and the simple metaphors that are also found there (for example, new wine in old wineskins, Matt. 9:17). John's method is to have Jesus employ longer and more complex metaphors for which it seems the word "allegory" is most descriptive. In John 10 we encounter the first of several of these allegories.

First, there comes a relatively simple allegory. It is the shepherd (the owner of the sheep) who enters by the door to the sheepfold, and the thieves who climb over the fence to gain access to the sheep. The sheep know their shepherd's voice, and he calls them by their individual names. The sheep follow him and not the others, because they know his voice (10:1–5). The point is simple. Jesus is the true leader of the people (the believers), and they know him, as he knows them. Consequently, they will follow him. This is in contrast to those who try to lead the people but fail because they are not the true revealer but blind guides.

The listeners hear this allegory but do not understand, and their misunderstanding occasions Jesus' expansion on the simple allegory. Actually, however, what follows as the explanation is in many ways more complex than the initial allegory. There are two somewhat different allegories used to explain the first—10:7–10 and 11–16. In the first Jesus is the door to the good pasture, through which persons must pass to find the abundant life of belief (which is another way of saying eternal life). The contrast with the false leaders is continued. They are the ones who try to mislead the believers. But the believers do not follow them, because they do not recognize the truth in them.

In the second additional allegory (10:11–17) Jesus is the "good shepherd," as opposed to others (hired helpers) who do not own the sheep and will not protect them. In contrast to the religious leaders, Jesus cares so much for his believers that he will lay down his life for them (John's subtle prediction of the passion). In vv. 14 and 15 the point of the entire group of allegories is made with a comparison of all-inclusive personal knowledge: The relationship between Jesus and the believers is parallel to the relationship between Jesus and the Father.

One point should emerge clearly from this mosaic of allegories. Believers belong by nature to the one who reveals the Father. John has piled comparison on comparison to contrast the legitimate ownership of the believers by Jesus with the illegitimate and destruc-

tive claims of the religious leaders. It is also clear that the false leaders
are all those who would lead the people away from their relationship
with God in Christ. The verbal pictures hammer at this single point
again and again but with ever-widening implications: First, the contrast is simply between the true shepherd who enters by the gate and
the false leaders who enter by climbing over the fence. Then, finally,
the contrast is between the more profoundly different religious leaders who flee from the people once they are threatened and the good
shepherd who will protect his believers even to the point of giving up
his life.

The last of the allegories is followed by a brief discourse which is
very important, for it picks up the commitment of Jesus to die for his
followers and expands it. The brief discourse in 10:17–18 makes one
poignant point: Jesus' absolutely autonomous decision to give up his
life. No one forces the act of his love. That decision is in harmony
with the Father's will, and it will eventually involve the return of
Jesus' life to the Father. This concise statement is a summary of the
Johannine view of the cross which we will find acted out in the passion story.

The discourse is followed, predictably, by a radical division between those who believe the speaker and those who do not. Again we
have the claim that Jesus is possessed by a demon and the counter-
charge that one possessed by a demon could not open the eyes of the
blind (10:19–21). John will not allow us to rest for long from his
persistent message that the revelation of the Father causes a great
fracturing of humanity.

We might say that what follows is more of the same. The conflict
with the leaders, which we have seen again and again and on which
the allegories are focused, in one way continues (10:22–39). John
reminds us that Jesus is again in the temple, suggesting that the reader
remember Jesus is in the midst of opposition. With that setting in mind
a dialogue ensues: "Tell us if you are the Messiah." "I have already
told you, and I have done works which should answer your question." Jesus then proceeds to discuss unbelief in terms of the allegory
of the sheep and shepherd. The thrust of this is that some persons are
Jesus' sheep, and for that reason they listen and follow him. They
belong to him, and they are given eternal life by him. These words
summarize and reiterate the earlier allegory of the sheep and

shepherd (10:1–18) as well as reemphasize its central message: Some are the sheep of Jesus and some are not. Unbelief then arises from those who are not part of the revealer's flock (10:22–29).

In suddenly going to the heart of the matter to answer the question of his identity Jesus claims that the Father and the Son are one (10:30). The response is an attempt to stone him. Another brief dialogue takes place: "Why do you stone me?" "Because you are claiming to be God." Jesus' subsequent defense of himself takes three forms. First, he defends himself by reference to Scripture (specifically Ps. 82:6)— those to whom God has given his message are called gods. Second, his defense is made on the basis of his identity—Jesus is chosen and sent by the Father. Finally, Jesus defends himself on the basis of his works—he does the works of God. The conclusion is that the Father is in the Son and the Son in the Father. Predictably again, the response is hostile. They try to arrest him. The section concludes with Jesus' retreating from the area along with those who believe in him. In spite of the emphasis of this section on the opposition to Jesus and the lengthening of the shadow of the cross along Jesus' way, the concluding verse reads, "And many believed in him there" (that is, beyond the Jordan where the Baptizer had worked).

SUMMARY

It is now clear that John has wanted us to see the inevitable unbelief with which Jesus is met when he goes to the home court of the opponents—Jerusalem and the temple. The revelation of God goes to the very heart of that which humanity holds dear, in this case, their religious establishment. Hence, it is inevitable that the revealing of divine truth is met with resistance and opposition. The vital message of this Gospel, as unpleasant as it may be, is that there can be no revelation that does not in some way evoke a response of unbelief.

But the emphasis upon that theme makes all the more marvelous the counterpoint of John's story: There is belief even amid the rejection. The hinge of the first half of the Gospel which we found in chapter 6 swings the narrative into the paradoxical affirmation that faith stands precariously surrounded on every front by unbelief. It is that tension between faith and unbelief, between faith stranded on an island in a sea of unbelief, which John has forced us to comprehend in these last three chapters.

4
The Die Is Cast

11:1—12:50

One must be careful in labeling chapters 11—12 as John's transition from the first of his grand themes (the revelation of glory in Jesus) to the second (the glory that God gives Jesus in the passion). The truth is, of course, that the chapters do provide that necessary transitional link, but they are nonetheless markedly significant in themselves. While steering the reader's attention to the climax of the Gospel, they are themselves the penultimate climax and a fitting conclusion of the first twelve chapters.

THE EMINENT SIGN AND ITS
BASE CONSEQUENCE: SEVENTH SIGN (11:1–57)

Like the unfolding of a great classical tragedy, the inevitability of the death of Jesus at the hands of the religious leaders flows ever so predictably from the previous chapters. But in a sense John reaches that final act by means of a startling narrative. He has shown us again and again that the wondrous acts of Jesus invariably result in division among the witnesses. What John is about to tell us is that the most marvelous of Jesus' signs—the raising from the dead of one who had been entombed four days—is the act that provokes the decision to plot the death of Jesus. That sign, which reveals glory as perhaps none other, also reveals the depth of human deprivation!

In 11:1–4 John quickly prepares us for what is to come in the climax of the story. First, he introduces the characters involved in the story:

Mary, Martha, and Lazarus, Jesus is then informed of the illness of
Lazarus, a dear friend. Jesus' response to the news is frightfully
disappointing. John has Jesus indicate to us the eventual outcome of
this illness—it will be a means by which God's presence will once
again be affirmed (v. 4). But we are then told that, even though Jesus
loved Lazarus and his sisters, he loitered where he was for two days
after receiving the news of his friend's illness. Jesus finally decides to
return to Judea—at least to the region of Bethany where his friend lies
dying. Through the lips of the disciples John reminds us of the dangers
awaiting Jesus in that region, so that the terrible result of the sign is
anticipated for us. The words on the lips of Thomas the twin (v. 16)
draw the even further distant future into the present. "Let us go with
Jesus *that we may die with him!*"

Jesus alerts his followers that Lazarus is in a sleep from which only
God's power can awaken him, but they fail to comprehend what Jesus
means; so their master must frankly tell them—Lazarus is dead
(11:11–15). Jesus knows precisely what conditions will confront him
in Bethany and precisely what he will do and what will transpire.
Although his followers have witnessed his marvels many times, they
cannot imagine what Jesus has in mind. His sovereignty stands con-
trasted with the slow, plodding manner in which humans learn.
Hence, in John's introduction to the story (11:1–16) he has set up the
dramatic conditions for the sign—Jesus' delay in going to Bethany,
his sovereign lordship over the conditions of life, the disciples' lack of
awareness of what is to happen, but (perhaps most important) their
sense of the danger awaiting them and their master in that region.

Lazarus has been in the grave four days, an implicit assertion that
from the human point of view he is indeed dead (11:17). Recognizing
the conditions that sometimes appear to be death, the Jews believed
that the spirit of the deceased person hovered about the tomb for three
days beyond death, hence making possible within that time what we
today would call a resuscitation. But Lazarus is truly dead and hope
of his recovery gone. The scene, therefore, is one of mourning, with
friends and family gathered to comfort one another (v. 19).

The conversation with Martha (11:20–27) is an interpretation before the fact of what is about to happen. Martha first affirms her faith
that Jesus might have prevented her brother's death had he been
there—a statement of faith, to be sure, but with a barb that implies
Jesus is responsible for the death. Still, she is confident that Jesus can

bring divine intervention. Martha is portrayed as one whose faith is strong but as yet incomplete. Jesus promises her that her brother will live, and Martha responds with an affirmation of her belief in the resurrection of the dead, although one can almost hear a tone of irrelevance in her confession—Lazarus will be raised on the last day, but that is little help for the moment. Martha has responded with a bit of hope for the last day—what God will do on that climactic final episode of human history. But Jesus' startling words move the conversation from the distant future and what will transpire then to the present and what *is* transpiring in the person of God's revealer. *Jesus is the resurrection*; where he is, there is conquest over the power of death, and belief in him transforms the reality of death into the life that is not bounded by death (v. 25).

When Martha's true but immature faith is challenged by Jesus' statement and his question, "Do you believe this?" her answer is a confession of who Jesus is. Through Martha's confession John is leading us to see the point: What matters in the face of death is who you believe this Jesus to be. The question of death is really a question of Jesus' identity (indeed, all ultimate questions for John are a single question of Jesus' identity).

It is surely to build the dramatic quality of the story, to enhance the eager anticipation of the reader, that John stresses that Jesus remains where he is—again!—while Martha goes to inform Mary of his arrival. Mary echoes Martha's first greeting (11:32). Her weeping and the mourning of those with her, as well as the sight of the tomb itself, contribute to the strong emotions felt by Jesus. We may not comprehend all that John intends us to understand by the fact that Jesus weeps (v. 35) and is deeply moved (vv. 33, 38). Were his feelings expressions of bereavement, a sympathy for those others who were mourning, anger at the sight of the way death has distorted and disfigured human existence, or some combination of these? Whatever may have been the meaning John intends for us to grasp, this much is sure: The sense of the tragic in human existence pervades even a situation in which the glory of God is about to be revealed. The reality of death is certain, even when faith in Christ enables one to move through death to life.

John's dramatic narrative continues (11:39–44): Remove the stone! But the reality of death means that the body has already begun to decompose. Even Jesus' prayer is for dramatic effect, for he already knows what God will do through him. With the sovereign command to "Come out!" death yields to its Lord, and Lazarus emerges from the tomb still bound with the death clothes. The final command of Jesus that Lazarus be unbound and allowed to go is impregnated with symbolic meaning, for the whole thrust of the narrative is that Christ is the liberator, freeing humanity from all the powers that oppress and bind.

The marvelous sign has been accomplished! In his sovereign power Christ has demonstrated what it means that he is the resurrection and the life.The narrative transmits two inseparable points to the reader. First, there is a radical new beginning that God is effecting in Christ—a beginning that subordinates even the power of death to God's rule. But, second, this eminent sign among the signs narrated in John 1—12 anticipates still another "sign." The resurrection of Lazarus cannot help but point the reader on to Jesus' own resurrection.

But the "eminent sign" is followed by a strange consequence. The Pharisees determine that Jesus must die but not without some discussion. Their fear is that these mighty works will gather a crowd of followers around Jesus, and the Romans will view the movement as a revolution and destroy the people and the temple (11:48). John's irony here is evident from the vantage point of a post–A.D. 70 date, for, even though Jesus is put to death, the Romans still destroyed the nation and the temple. The ironic quality of the passage continues as Caiaphas insists that it is better for one person to die than for the nation to be destroyed. John explains the irony of the high priest's words in an aside (11:51–52)—Jesus is to die to save the nation from its death.

The die is cast! The eminent sign yields a base consequence understandable only in the light of John's persistent exposition of the darkness of the world and the blindness of humanity.

PREPARING JESUS FOR HIS DEATH AND ANOTHER DEATH PLOT (12:1–11)

The incongruity of the religious establishment is highlighted again in chapter 12 and the death plot against Lazarus. This second death plot unites the narratives of John 11 and 12. In chapter 11 the resurrection of Lazarus previews the resurrection of Jesus, even as it determines his death. In chapter 12 the anointing of his body prepares Jesus for his death and burial, and this act too is followed by a death plot—this one against Lazarus.

Mary's act of anointing (12:1-3) is the act of one filled with love and gratitude. In chapter 11 John has Mary's sister, Martha, show how a disciple's faith grows and matures in relationship with Christ. Here Mary symbolizes the disciple's love of her master. Taken together, Martha and Mary constitute a corporate image of the true follower of Jesus. But Mary's act is also one that points beyond itself to what is to come. With the cross lurking in the shadowy corner of the near future, the anointing of his feet prepares Jesus for his burial.

Lest there be any doubt that John wants his readers to see the future through the lens of this act, Judas is now characterized for what he is and for what he will do (12:4-6). John intends no character analysis of Judas. But he does intend for us to see that Satan's use of Judas is made possible by a tragic character flaw—his basic dishonesty. In another sense Judas's appearance at this point in the narrative poses the negative figure of discipleship (Judas) over against the positive figure (Mary and Martha).

Lazarus poses still a further threat to the religious leaders, for people are swarming out to see this marvel, a man who was once dead and now lives. As a symbol of the eminent sign of Jesus' identity, Lazarus is evoking belief in Jesus, which in turn weakens the power and authority of the religious leaders. So, another death plot is laid out. Like Jesus, Lazarus must be put to death, lest his very presence fan the fires of a new faith which the status quo cannot tolerate. In connection with the beautiful act of love and devotion of Mary, there stands still another base intent. For our evangelist the two sides of human existence are welded together—sight and faith, on the one hand, blindness and unbelief, on the other.

THE ENTRY INTO JERUSALEM AND THE JUDGMENT OF THE WORLD (12:12-50)

The motif of unbelief alongside of discipleship is the dominant theme in the conclusion to the first section of this Gospel. The remainder of chapter 12 is another concise narrative followed by a discourse. The narrative which sets the stage for the last public discourse of Jesus is the entry into Jerusalem. It is called by some a "triumphal" entry, but for John the emphasis is less on the triumph than on the dreadfulness of Jesus' public appearance at the heart of the opponents' territory. It is no coincidence that entry into Jerusalem should be followed by a discussion of the judgment of the world, for in a sense Jerusalem symbolizes the unbelief and hostility of the world. The evangelist has told us of the danger that awaits Jesus in the holy city, so that danger saturates the superficially joyful atmosphere of the entry scene (12:12–16). The crowd that meets Jesus acts without full knowledge of what they are doing. They are there because of the marvelous deed this Jesus has done in Lazarus's resurrection (v. 17). Yet they are correct in that they welcome him as their King. Their King he is; but in a much different sense than they imagine. The disciples, John tells us in another of his asides, will understand this act of Jesus' entry into Jerusalem on a donkey only after Jesus has been enthroned by God as King in the crucifixion-resurrection (v. 16). The Pharisees epitomize the lack of human perception when they are made to say with typical Johannine irony, "The whole world is coming to him!" (v. 19). Indeed, the whole world will come to Jesus, but not now, not in this mob scene of immature faith, but after the King has been enthroned.

What the Pharisees unknowingly express in their words is now enacted when the "Greeks" attempt to come to Jesus. John introduces the Greeks at this point for purely symbolic reasons, it appears, for they do not figure in the narrative or in the following discourse (at least directly). Their function here (as well perhaps as their indirect access to Jesus through the disciples) prefigures the coming of the Gentile world to the Christian faith in the life of the early church. It is this hint of universalism heralded in advance of the world mission of the church that occasions the solemn announcement of 12:23—this is the "hour." That act by which God gives Jesus the glory that is his and that makes possible the turning of the Gentiles to him, the "drawing" of all persons to him, has begun (12:32).

How that glorification of Jesus is to take place is now declared clearly and openly. In the words of Jesus regarding the way in which a seed must die in order to give birth to the life of the plant, the way of glorification is laid out (12:24). In connection with the drawing of that path, the course of the followers of Christ is also charted. Jesus' total devotion to the Father makes it impossible for one to follow him without a comparable total devotion. That devotion is forcibly expressed in the insistence that followers of Jesus must "hate" their own lives in order to serve Christ and gain the Father's honor for themselves.

The tragic path to the Father's glory, however, is one which extracts pain, even for the Father's unique Son. In 12:27–28 we hear the man Jesus agonizing over the course his life must now take. The triumph of the entry into Jerusalem, the eagerness of the masses to be identified with him, and even the attraction of the Greeks are tempered with these excruciating words! The only hope is that this "hour" of suffering death will result in the glorification of God. That hope is confirmed in the heavenly voice which promises that God will give glory to this suffering one in the future. This human agony in the face of death is, however, immediately balanced by the divine sovereignty of Jesus as he says that the heavenly voice was not for his sake but the crowd's (v. 30).

The dire consequences of the act of Jesus' receiving the Father's glory are now announced. In the discussion-discourse unfolded in 12:29–50 the motif of judgment is articulated as the result of the glorification of Christ. The crowd is, of course, divided among themselves as to the voice from heaven. Some recognize it as God's confirmation of his Son, but others claim they heard only thunder. Jesus explains that his crucifixion-enthronement (his being "lifted up") will overthrow the forces of evil and win humanity to himself; but the crowd misunderstands again, wondering how the Messiah could suffer such humiliation as crucifixion. They cannot believe in spite of all that Jesus has done. It is as if God has blinded them from the truth. And John here repeats the common motif that unbelief is due to God's act. And if the people do believe (John says of the religious leaders), they do so in private, afraid of the consequences of their belief. (John may intend a reference here to the "closet believers" like Nicodemus and Joseph of Arimathea. Compare 19:38–39.)

John brings chapter 12 to a magnificent conclusion with a brief discourse that enlarges the themes of judgment and life (12:44–50). Jesus again declares that humans have the opportunity to believe and to see the Father in him. His presence is not for judgment but for the bestowal of real, authentic life (eternal life; see 3:17). His presence calls for a decision, it would seem. He is light in the darkness, and those who see the light and embrace it pass beyond judgment. Those who reject the light in favor of the darkness are doomed to judgment (which here as often in John is the equivalent of condemnation). To obey the Father is followed by eternal life, and obedience is to believe that Jesus is indeed the light of God in this world of darkness.

SUMMARY

In that ever-so-brief speech John concludes the first half of the story and leads us forward—to the passion. The solemn words of Jesus that unbelief yields judgment, while belief preserves one in eternal life, fix the tragedy of the human refusal to find God in his revealer. In this section, the die is cast for the earthly life of the revealer. The sober reality of blindness and unbelief that haunts chapters 1—12 is now finished in the decision to put Jesus to death. Even while the reality of belief and its consequence, eternal life, are present, the inescapable presence of unbelief and its consequence, judgment, are made undeniable.

John leads us to understand the wonder of what God is about to do in Christ. In the cross the darkness of the world will do its best to snuff out the intrusive light. But its very act of so doing is the means by which God will glorify his Son. The logic of the story John tells is a contorted logic. It is a logic that finds the glorification of Jesus in the act of those who intended the very opposite. For that reason the overwhelming reality of darkness and unbelief has dominated John 2—12. It is the darkness of the world that will eventually point the world to the light. And so, if it is the case that John understands the unbelief of the world rooted in God's action (as 12:39–41 may indicate), it is by means of unbelief that God in Christ makes belief possible. Jesus has revealed God's glory with the result that he is about to be put to death. Now in the course of that death he is to receive God's glory.

PART TWO:
JESUS RECEIVES GLORY
13:1—20:29

5

Love and

Rejection

13:1-38

The first part of the Gospel (chaps. 2—12) focused our attention on the horizontal meaning of God's act in Christ. The glory of God has been mediated through a man who lived among humans. The second part (chaps. 13—20) adjusts the focus of our attention on the vertical dimension of John's story of Jesus. What we will learn, of course, is that the difference between the horizontal and vertical focuses is only a matter of emphasis.

John's narrative progresses smoothly from chapters 11 and 12 into the preface of the passion narrative. If those chapters have made us vividly conscious of the base reaction of humans to the divine Word of God, chapter 13 poses that fact again—in a new way and in a new setting. John 13 is comprised of two pairs of narratives, each of which gives expression to divine love, on the one hand, and human failure, on the other. By these pairs John draws our attention to the last words Jesus shares with his disciples before his crucifixion (chaps. 14—17).

FOOT WASHING AND BETRAYAL (13:1-30)

The narrative of the foot washing is shocking. The setting is the day before the Passover, which suggests that the grand event of God's liberation of the people of Israel is in some way a foreshadowing of the meaning of God's act in Christ. Jesus and the disciples are gathered for their evening meal. Jesus is acutely aware of the approaching hour when he would return to his Father and his love for those who are "his own" in this world (13:1). It is that sense of destiny and love that epitomizes these narratives as well as those in chapters 14—17. But the foot-washing narrative itself is mixed with the ingredient of betrayal which is also part of Jesus' consciousness (13:2). The announcement of Judas's betrayal is anticipated in 13:2 and its significance implied with the statement that it is the satanic power that uses Judas as an instrument for his work. (This is John's only use of the word "Satan.")

In this atmosphere Jesus proceeds to wash the feet of the disciples with water and to dry them with a towel. John does not elaborate this simple act (13:4–5). It is an act that speaks for itself without elaboration. John means for us to view the act in its bare but powerful simplicity. The one who is the revealer of God among humans undertakes the act of supreme servanthood, indeed, supreme love.

John's narrative then explores the twin meanings of Jesus' act. The first meaning arises out of the conversation between Jesus and Peter, as Jesus attempts to wash Peter's feet (13:6–11). Peter appropriately enough tries to deny Jesus his humble act. Jesus tells Peter that the act he is doing will become clear at a later time. But Peter still resists the act. Jesus must declare that one is a disciple only if he or she has experienced the cleansing act of Jesus' love (v. 6). Now Peter wants to be washed all over! In Jesus' response (vv. 10–11) the act he performs is a divine cleansing of those who have been with him all this time, and through this time have already experienced cleansing, all except one (and the betrayal intrudes its ugly face into the narrative once again).

But the meaning of the act is stated, second, in the discourse that follows (13:12–20). Jesus tells his disciples exactly what he intended in this act. It is an example of servant lordship. Jesus is their Lord and master, to be sure, but look at what kind of a master he is! His lordship is a lordship of love for them all, and so now the disciples have an example of that loving behavior that can instruct them in their discipleship. They are not greater than their master, and, if their master has so treated them, they must treat others. Jesus' promise to Peter that he will later understand the act of foot washing is John's way of showing us that this symbolic act of love presages the meaning of the cross where Jesus' supreme act of love will be affirmed as the glory of

God present in this world. 13:19 underscores that predicted reality, for what is about to happen (the cross) will shout the divine affirmation, "I AM," to all the cosmos.

This powerful deed of love is now set beside the most dreadful deed of betrayal (13:21–30). What John wants the reader to *feel*—in narrating the prediction of Judas's terrible deed—is the horror of being betrayed by one with whom you have shared table fellowship. The narrative itself is unadorned. Jesus predicts that one of his own will betray him and passes on to Judas the bit of bread dipped in the sauce. At the very moment that Jesus is extending his love and friendship to Judas, Satan overpowers his victim. Evil functions in the midst of the most intimate of relationships. Jesus knows what will transpire (v. 21) and even permits the evil plan to unfold in his sovereign act of handing the bread to Judas (v. 27) and urging him "to get it over with" (v. 28). To all of this the other disciples seem blinded (vv. 28–29). We need not puzzle over how this could be, especially given Jesus' identification of the betrayer in v. 26. It is the tragic naiveté of the disciples John wants us to grasp.

The narrative and discourse confront us with a pair of realities (the foot washing, on the one hand, and the betrayal, on the other) that captures the meaning of the Jesus story—divine love expressed concretely and vividly only to be answered by the reality of human evil. The next section of chapter 13 will repeat that point like the master theme of a great symphony.

THE LOVE COMMANDMENT AND DENIAL (13:31–38)

Love and rejection dominate the story of the foot washing and announcement of Judas's betrayal, and they will now dominate the next pair of units. Jesus begins to speak of his passion (13:31–32) immediately after Judas's departure. The betrayer is not privy to the mysterious meaning of Jesus' death and resurrection. Now Jesus speaks of himself as the Son of Man, for throughout the Gospels the Son of Man title is used of Jesus in his own speeches when the passion is under discussion (for example, Mark 8:31 and parallels in Matthew and Luke). Jesus first speaks of his glorification as a past event (13:31) and then as a future event (v. 32), suggesting the meaning of Jesus'

ministry in chapters 1—12 and the meaning of his passion in the
second half of the Gospel. On the brink of his "departure" from
among the disciples (John's way of speaking of Jesus' death, resurrection, and ascension) Jesus issues the new commandment that they
love one another as he has loved them. This love for one another is
what will inform the world of their discipleship. We should note in
passing that the love commanded by Jesus is a love modeled on his
attitude toward the disciples. What is new about the commandment is
that the disciples have a specific example after which to pattern their
love.

Posed over against the commandment to love stands another instance of human depravity (13:36–38). Peter is sure that he can follow
Jesus wherever his master may go, and is bold enough even to claim
that he is willing and ready to die for Jesus. What a shocking contrast
is Jesus' prediction that Peter will deny his master three times before
the rooster has heralded the dawn of a new day. Human intent stands
in bitter contrast to actual behavior!

SUMMARY

Again a statement of love followed by an instance of human failure!
The two pairs of units (the foot washing with the announcement of the
betrayal and the love commandment with the prediction of denial)
pose the agonizing dissimilarity of the divine and human. The tragedy
of John's story of Jesus is well put in this manner of expressing his
point in a dialectical fashion. So very often his dialectical style is a
way of posing the encounter of the divine and human and the resultant
tragedy of that encounter. We have only to see how that tragedy
unfolds in the passion story itself, for John has now informed us of
what will transpire. But first we are privileged to enter into the privacy
of Jesus' relationship with his disciples to hear his parting words to
them.

6

Parting Words

14:1—17:26

Chapters 14—17 read like the last will and testament of Jesus—his last opportunity to help the disciples understand what they are experiencing. In the tradition of mighty leaders who are about to leave their followers (see for example the parting words of Moses in the last chapters of Deuteronomy) John has Jesus give a farewell speech. The logic of these words at this juncture in the plot is clear enough, standing as they do on the verge of the crucifixion. The inner logic of the discourses is, however, less clear. We cannot hide the fact of the constant repetition of ideas in these chapters and even the occasional contradiction with which the careful reader is faced. And yet John wanted his readers to hear those themes again and again. Perhaps the best way to allow them to speak with clarity is to assume that there is not to be found among these discourses a systematic logical development moving in one direction. They may better be thought of as an elliptical movement than as straight-line logic.

There are three major divisions among chapters 14—17, which betray a limited systematization within the discourses: the departure of Jesus and its consequences (chap. 14); the disciples' posture residing in Jesus and the world at the same time (chap. 15—16); and the final prayer of Jesus (chap. 17).

JESUS' DEPARTURE AND ITS CONSEQUENCES (14:1–31)

The final words of Jesus begin with a discussion of the "way" of Jesus' departure and of the disciples' "way" to the Father. Jesus is leaving his disciples, but by virtue of his presence and glorification the disciples have a way of knowing the Father. Jesus begins with a promise that meets the fear and anxiety his departure arouses. The promise is twofold: Jesus will prepare a place of residence with the Father (14:1–2)—the disciples have the promise of a heavenly home. The other promise is that Jesus will not be separated from the disciples forever. He will return to take the disciples to their heavenly place (v. 3). In these promises the departure of Jesus from his disciples is featured as a crisis of faith, to be sure, but a crisis for which they may be prepared.

Jesus' suggestion that the disciples know the way Jesus is about to take evokes the first admission of ignorance from the disciples. Thomas insists that they do not know the way Jesus is going. To this question Jesus replies that he himself is the way, as well as the truth and the life. All three terms seem to mean essentially the same thing—Jesus is the revelation of the Father and hence the only way by which humans can relate to God. To know Christ is to know the Father and to see Jesus is to see the Father (14:5–8).

Those words evoke the second admission of ignorance from the disciples. Philip must ask that Jesus show them the Father. Jesus' response (14:9–14) in summary suggests that the Father resides in Jesus and Jesus resides in the Father. John here repeats a major theme we have encountered earlier and one which will continue to appear in these parting words of Jesus, namely, abiding in, remaining in, or residing in (*menein*). This passage establishes the fact that there is a reciprocal residing between the Father and the Son; its implications are soon to be spelled out for the disciples. Because of this mutual residing, the words and acts of Jesus are the words and acts of the Father. The works alone that he does are enough to demonstrate this relationship. The theme of the work of Christ leads to the promise that the disciples too will be empowered to do the works of God—a result of their master's departure to be with the Father.

The crisis of faith resulting from Jesus' departure is answered, as we have seen, by the promise that Jesus will come again to take the disciples to their residence with the Father. But now another promise is given—this to assure the disciples that they are not deprived of the presence of God until such time that Jesus returns. That presence of God is the Paraclete (translated "Counselor," "Helper," or "Advocate"). In 14:15–18 we encounter the first of five statements made of the Paraclete. (See the comparative chart on p. 75.) In this passage the disciples are promised that the Spirit of God (the Paraclete) will reside with them forever and will not leave them as Jesus (the first "Paraclete") must.

But now attention shifts back again to the promise that Jesus will return to his disciples (14:18). The disciples will see Jesus again and then be assured that he resides with the Father. The mutual residing, however, is now expanded to include the fact that the disciples will be in Jesus and Jesus in them (v. 20). The mutual residing seems to refer to a relationship of the most intimate kind. The close relationship that Jesus enjoys with the Father is a model of the kind of singular relationship the disciples can expect with Jesus.

Again there is an abrupt transition to another set of ideas, these focused on the theme of obedience to the commandments of Jesus. Obedience to those commands assures believers that they are loved by the Father. But love of the Son also brings the love of the Father. A disciple called Judas, not Iscariot the betrayer, asks the question concerning how Jesus can reveal himself to the disciples but not to the world, which evokes the repetition of the themes just mentioned but now with an additional point: Love leads to obedience and obedience to love. The Father will reside in the one who loves and obeys Christ. Hence the third strand of the mutual residing theme is laid out—the Father's residing in the disciples. The antithesis sums up what has been said: One who does not love Jesus does not obey him. But what is the commandment spoken of in these verses? There is only one explicit commandment found on the lips of Jesus, and that is the love commandment in 13:34 and 15:12. The other imperative found frequently on the lips of Jesus is the command to believe in him and in the truth that the Father has sent him (for example, 14:11). The obedience Jesus demands from his disciples is then simply that they believe in him and love one another; and that constitutes for John all the imperative there need be for Christian faith and life.

The second of the passages regarding the Paraclete appears at this point (14:26). Here the promise is that the Paraclete will teach the disciples "all things" and enable them to remember all that Jesus has said. Again the role of the Paraclete saying is to offer comfort and reassurance. (See the chart on p. 75.)

Abruptly another theme is introduced: Peace. But this theme is tied

to the one that introduced this chapter. The disciples need not fear
Jesus' departure, for he gives them his peace—a peace which goes
beyond all that the world can give (14:27). Actually they should be
glad because Jesus is going to the Father. When this occurs (that is,
his death and resurrection) Jesus' departure will evoke their faith.
John understands these parting words, it appears, as preparation for
the passion, so that the suffering, death, and resurrection can be
viewed in faith and can evoke faith.

The sobering fact of the work of evil in the passion story concludes
chapter 14—the time for instructing the disciples is short. The last
words of v. 31 suggest that chapter 14 was once the totality of the
parting words of Jesus. But John invites us to consider some of the
same themes in a different way in chapters 15 and 16.

RESIDING IN JESUS AND IN
THE WORLD (15:1—16:33)

The themes of mutual residing that we found in chapter 14 begin the
new section in the form of the allegory of the vine and the branches
(15:1–6). Jesus is the vine, the disciples the branches, and the Father
the gardener. Residing in Jesus is like a branch acquiring its life from
the body of the vine. Faithfulness in life is like a vine branch bearing
fruit; on the other hand, unfaithfulness results in being sheared off the
vine and cast into the fire to burn. It is a simple allegory that makes the
most of the idea of residing in Jesus. The disciples are to reside in
Jesus as he resides in them, and then they will bear fruit. Failure to
reside in Jesus as he resides in them will mean the loss of life. Residing
in Jesus, v. 7 reveals, is allowing the words of Jesus to reside in you.
By residing in Jesus and bearing fruit (loving one another), the glory
(the presence) of the Father is shown. 15:9 speaks of residing in Jesus
in another way—in his love. But residing in Jesus' love means obey-
ing his commandments, just as Jesus' residing in the Father has meant
that he obey the Father and reside in his Father's love (v. 10). The
multiple dimensions of "residing in" have been fully exploited by
John.

In this ever-expanding spiral of thoughts, joy is now introduced as a
step beyond the peace that Jesus promises in 13:27. It is a joy that the
disciples have from Jesus' own joy. Quickly the theme of joy fades

into the theme of love once again (15:12–17). The commandment to love one another found at 13:34 is here repeated in only slightly different words. But the love commanded is here described in several differing ways. First, it is a love that is willing to give up life itself for the beloved. This extreme of love is the content of the comparison of the disciples' love to Jesus' own love. Jesus' love will soon demonstrate its own extremity. But, second, this is a love that transcends the relationship of master and servant to create a relationship of friendship. Jesus is the friend of the disciples and not only their master. This is so because the disciples know what Jesus is doing (15:12–15). Mutual love dissolves all ties of obligation and duty to form ties of affection and devotion. When one understands the extreme love of the cross, such a transformation results.

John will not, however, allow us to forget that this relationship between the disciples and Jesus stands in sharp opposition to the world, the realm of unbelief. The world hates the believer, for the believer has been taken from his or her life in the world to a relationship with Christ, with the result that believers no longer belong to the world (15:18–19). This is the case because the world will persecute the disciples just as it persecutes Jesus. The world is responsible for its unbelief because of the revelation in Christ (v. 22). In hating Christ the world hates the Father and brings guilt upon itself. John concludes this brief discussion of the opposition of the world with an Old Testament citation from the Psalms (35:19 and/or 69:4), accusing the world of hating Jesus for no reason (15:20–25).

The third Paraclete passage appears at this point, but why here is not clear. The Paraclete comes from the Father to speak of the Son, even as the disciples are asked to speak about the Son (15:26–27).

The opposition of the world is revived immediately in chapter 16. This time the topic is persecution itself and perhaps martyrdom. The believers will be excluded from the synagogue by those who think that they are doing God a favor in expelling Christians. Jesus tells them these things to prepare them for the time when it will happen, even though it brings sadness (16:1–6).

The fourth and fifth Paraclete sayings stand back to back beginning with 16:7 and continuing through 16:14. The chart on p. 75 summarizes simply what is said of the Paraclete throughout these chapters. Note several of the chart's features. First, the Paraclete serves as a substitute for the presence of Christ and continues to keep Christ's word in mind and even leads the believers to "all truth." Second, the Paraclete functions primarily among the community of believers but is also responsible for convicting the hostile world of its unbelief. Third, the Paraclete comes from the Father and from the Son and functions to bring glory to Christ. Obviously John wants the reader to know of the continued work of God in the Spirit but also to know how the Spirit is rooted in the revelation of God in Christ.

In the process of separation from a loved one there is often mourning and rejoicing at the same time. Just so, says John, is the experience of the separation from Christ. In 16:16–22 Jesus speaks of two short periods of time. It will be only a short time until the disciples will grieve over Jesus' departure; but it will be only another short time until Jesus comes again to the disciples and makes them glad. Then their sadness will be changed to gladness, just as the suffering to bring forth a child is followed by gladness and joy. It appears that the first short period of time refers to the time until the crucifixion, and the second short period of time is the time between the crucifixion and resurrection. It is then that the disciples will understand what is going on and will not need to ask questions of their master, as they have throughout the parting words. Similarly, Jesus will no longer speak with mysterious, veiled language but with clarity. That day is a time of gladness and insight into the meaning of Christ's revelation (16:23–28).

The disciples think that they now understand and ironically claim that Jesus is no longer speaking in figures and that they now know Jesus is indeed from the Father. Jesus, however, must confront them with the fact that their enthusiasm is overly eager. The time is near when they will be scattered far and wide, leaving Jesus alone (even though he is never entirely alone). Finally, there is a grim reminder and an empowering promise: The world will mistreat the disciples and persecute them, but Jesus has overcome the forces of this world—the power of unbelief (16:29–33).

A FINAL PRAYER (17:1–26)

The final farewell words are a lengthy prayer in which much of chapters 14—16 is summarized and indeed much of the Gospel itself is drawn together. The prayer is a veritable collage of Johannine themes. As such it should be left so, lest it lose the power gained from the intermixing of themes and language. Still, there may be some value in pulling the collage apart to examine the parts, in order that those various parts might be appreciated all the more when they form a whole. For that purpose we will isolate two of the major themes woven together in John 17. In particular the prayer gives expression to the relationship of the Father and the Son and to the characteristics of the disciples.

Concerning the disciples, Jesus says: They have been given to him out of the world by the Father. They have been given the Father's message, and they obey the Father and know the relationship between the Father and the Son. They belong to the Father and not to the world. For that reason the world hates them, even though they are sent into the world. Jesus asks, then, that they be protected from the evil of the world, as he has guarded them thus far. The glory which is Jesus' is shown through them; in fact they are given the glory that is Jesus'. Jesus asks that they may be one, as the Father and Son are one, and that their unity may lead the world to know that the Father has sent the Son and that the Father loves the disciples. The prayer requests that they may mutually reside in the Father and in the Son as they are in one another. Not only the disciples of the historical Jesus are prayed for but also others who become disciples.

Interwoven with the threads concerning the disciples are those concerning the Son and his relationship with the Father. The Father glorifies the Son, and the Son glorifies the Father. The authority and message of the Father is given to the Son, including the gift of eternal life. The Father sent the Son, and it is the Father's work that the Son is given to do. The Son had the Father's glory and love before the world. The Son knows and reveals the Father. Indeed, the Father and the Son are one. The Son comes from the Father and has been given the power of the Father's name. All the Son has is the Father's, and all the Father has is the Son's. The Son finally goes to the Father.

The author of the Fourth Gospel has articulated these themes so that ideas appear to emerge from one another in the manner of a chain reaction: One idea produces another and that one still another, and so on. The result of this self-sustaining series is like a free association of ideas and themes. The collage is effective mainly because of the power of the words used by John. The chapter comes closer to poetry than discourse; it is more akin to religious meditation than systematic theology.

THEMES IN THE PARACLETE PASSAGES

14:15–17	14:26	15:26–27	16:7–11	16:12–14
Paraclete is sent by the Father at the Son's request. Paraclete is "another paraclete"—Jesus is first. Paraclete is "Spirit of Truth." Paraclete cannot be known by the world but only by believers. Paraclete resides with believers forever (unlike Jesus who must "go away").	Paraclete is the Holy Spirit. Paraclete is sent by the Father in Jesus' name. Paraclete teaches "all things." Paraclete helps the believers remember what Jesus has told them.	Paraclete is the Spirit of Truth. Paraclete comes from the Father. Paraclete is sent from the Father by Jesus. Paraclete speaks of Jesus. (Implied: Paraclete is related to the believers' witness to Jesus.)	Paraclete comes only because Jesus goes away. Paraclete is sent by Jesus. Paraclete convicts the world of sin, righteousness, and judgment (that is, exposes sin of the world, its misconception of righteousness and judgment).	Paraclete is Spirit of Truth. Paraclete leads believers to all truth. Paraclete obediently speaks what is heard. Paraclete speaks of future things. Paraclete glorifies Jesus. Paraclete relays words of Son to believers.
EMPHASIS: *Paraclete fills the need of believers resulting from the departure of Jesus.*	EMPHASIS: *Work of Paraclete is within community of faith, keeping words of Jesus "fresh."*	EMPHASIS: *Paraclete is connected with the power of the witness of believers for Jesus.*	EMPHASIS: *Paraclete functions beyond community of faith by judging the world and demonstrating its wrong.*	EMPHASIS: *Paraclete leads believers even to all truth.*

SUMMARY

In chapters 14—17 all of John's thoughts have been blended together and empowered by means of their repetitious reappearances. For whatever reason these chapters stand together. They are not made powerless by their association; indeed, the opposite is the case. Their power derives from the way in which themes and related themes are repeated. In particular John has ever so patiently constructed his theme of mutual residing. In sum, we have been told that Jesus is in the Father and the Father in Jesus (14:10) and that the Father and the Son reside in the disciples (14:23). The disciples reside in Jesus, and Jesus in the disciples (15:4). Finally, it is claimed that the Paraclete resides in the disciples (14:17). If we add to this use of the concept of residing the simpler but equivalent expression that so-and-so is IN such-and-such, we find the theme intensified. The disciples are IN Jesus, as Jesus is IN the disciples (14:20). Jesus prays that the disciples might be IN God and IN the Son as the Son is IN the Father and the Father IN the Son (17:21).

John has portrayed a relationship of the believers with God and with Christ that is intentionally modeled after the relationship of the Father and the Son. In these parting words, the private teaching to the disciples as to what they must know before the passion, John's story of Jesus paints a scene of the nature and the life of the believer that arises from the nature of the revealer himself.

With the parting words spoken, the last scene before the final act is concluded, and the drama unfolds toward a tragic grand finale.

7

The Exaltation

18:1—20:29

The grand finale of John's story of Jesus is told with a keen sense of the dramatic power of the events and with a profound appreciation of the value of narrative as a means of conveying religious truth. It is, of course, the story of the passion that is presented to us in each of the Gospels, but now that story is told in the light of the majestic themes we have encountered in chapters 1—18. Perhaps the most important thing for us to realize as we move into the final act of this story is that, while Jesus as a human suffers and dies as all humans do, John's story of Jesus is the story of one who stands above humanity, even though he is among humans as well. In short, John's story of Jesus' passion is shot through with paradox, enigma, and impenetrable mystery!

THE BETRAYAL AND ARREST (18:1–11)

The tone of the betrayal that is so carefully pitched in 13:21–30 resounds here as Judas's plan is brought to completion. John does not elaborate the details of Judas's plan and how it is executed. It is enough for us to know that Jesus went to a garden which was a familiar place for him and the disciples, and it was there Judas brought the soldiers. Judas is called "the traitor" to enforce again the horrible deed he is doing. He and the soldiers come with torches and lanterns, trying to find their way in the darkness of their deed. 18:4 clearly reminds us, however, of who is in command here. Jesus knows what is about to transpire, and he even takes the initiative in addressing the arresting officers (much as he took the initiative in offering Judas the bread in 13:26). When they tell him that they are looking for Jesus of Nazareth, Jesus replies with those enigmatic words that identify him with the revelation of God, "I AM" (18:8, translated "I am he" for the sake of proper English). With the sound of these words the soldiers stagger backward and fall to the ground. The spoken words of this revealer are enough by themselves to level the opposition. Can there be any doubt that it is Jesus who controls his own arrest? Jesus helps the poor soldiers by asking them again who it is they seek and thus gives them a means of recovering from their devastated condition.

Jesus now speaks on behalf of his disciples: "I am the one you are to arrest; let these others go." Jesus' immediate concern is for his followers, which is what this whole passion narrative is about. John has told us (8:4) that Jesus knows what is to take place, and now he points out that Jesus is here fulfilling the words he spoke earlier. He had said (17:12) that those given to him by the Father had been carefully protected and preserved, except for one, Judas; and at his arrest he sees to it that not one of his followers is lost. Again, it is Jesus who controls the scene.

But brave Peter, who is willing to die to follow Jesus, strikes out in an almost comical effort to save his master. He cuts off the ear (earlobe?) of the High Priest's servant, Malchus, who is not one of the arresting officers but perhaps an innocent onlooker who had followed the crowd to the garden! Peter cannot even choose a proper object of his protective concern for Jesus! The well-intentioned act to defend his master is symbolic of the futility of human efforts amid events moved by powers beyond the human arena. Jesus' words to Peter are John's way of informing us that Jesus has willfully elected to undergo suffering—the final act of obedience. Using the image of the cup of suffering, Jesus affirms his acceptance of God's plan for this course of events.

Human will and power are of little significance in this scene. It is rather the will of the Father and the power of the Son that are front stage in this first episode of the passion drama. John shows us his main motif for the subsequent acts that make up the grand finale. The Son has another work to perform in the oneness of his obedience and love with the Father, and the Son determines his own destiny.

JESUS' TRIAL AND PETER'S (18:12—27)

John's story of the passion has a two-part trial which is familiar to us from the other Gospels—a hearing before religious leaders and a trial before the representative of the Roman Empire, Pilate. John's story of the religious trial is interspersed with the account of Peter's denial. Jesus is bound and taken to the father-in-law of the High Priest, and the former High Priest, himself, Annas. In 18:12–14 John does little more than set the stage for the trial and then cuts away rather quickly to the story of Peter. Peter has gained entrance into the courtyard of the High Priest by virtue of the presence of another (and mysterious) disciple who is well known to the religious authorities. The scene is set for the trial of Jesus *and* Peter!

Peter is immediately recognized as one of the disciples by a young woman at the gate. There he denies for the first time that he is one of Jesus' disciples. He then huddles around a fire with other servants and guards.

Jesus' hearing before the High Priest is short. He is asked about his teachings, and his defense is to say that he has taught publicly and those who have heard him can be questioned about the content of his teaching. He is promptly struck by one of the guards for his discourteous manner. Jesus responds that he has said nothing wrong or false. Without pause he is sent on to Caiaphas.

The scene shifts back to Peter in the courtyard, warming himself by the fire. Again he is asked if he is not one of Jesus' disciples, and again he denies his association with Jesus. Then a relative of the servant whose ear Peter had cut off asks for the last time, "Was it not you that I saw in the garden when they arrested him?" (How ironic that Peter's well-intentioned but futile act to defend Jesus should become the mark destined to convict him!) For the third and final time Peter denies his discipleship. The rooster sounds its morning alarm—the time has come!

It is Peter who is on trial here, not Jesus. More accurately, it is humanity on trial, humanity represented by the religious leaders and by poor Peter. The antiphonal telling of the two trials—Jesus' *and* Peter's—makes it clear that humanity is being charged and tried. While the innocent Jesus is being tried, it is Peter who is found guilty.

But the irony of John's tale also involves the religious leaders whose questions belie the issue and whose only charge against Jesus is discourtesy! Humanity is found guilty, but without even so much as a sigh of regret. The religious leaders have no idea what they are doing; and Peter does not shed a single tear after having so decisively surrendered his loyalty to Jesus!

PILATE AND JESUS (18:28—19:16)

John's account shows little interest in the religious leaders and their trial of Jesus, but a good deal of interest in Pilate and the political trial. In this passage we witness the collision of two arenas of human life and thought—the political and the religious. John carefully portrays this significant political leader, Pilate. The trial before Pilate is carefully told in eight scenes, alternating between those involving Pilate and the crowd and those dealing with Pilate and Jesus. A number of moods are detected in the movement from one scene to another. In each succeeding scene dealing with the crowd John portrays them as more and more desperate in their determination to have Jesus put to death. Pilate in turn becomes increasingly frightened and anxious as he sees the inevitable emerging before his eyes. Through it all Jesus remains passive in his sovereignty.

Scene one (18:28-32) depicts the initial encounter between Pilate and the crowd. The adversary relationship is immediately established as Pilate challenges the officials to state the charge against Jesus. Pilate's loathing of the Jewish crowd is implicit in this scene; but that loathing will shortly turn to respect and fear. The cry of the crowd that they must let Pilate handle the matter, for they do not have the power of capital punishment, alerts Pilate and the reader to the goal of the mob.

Scene two (18:33-38a) begins to weave the delicate relationship between Pilate and the accused: Powerful Rome toys with the unknown and strange Jesus in order to discover what sort of person this accused is. Pilate straight away raises the question of Jesus' kingship. Is Jesus foolish enough to test the sovereign right of Rome? The contention over kingship proves that Pilate has no notion of Jesus' authority. In spite of Jesus' efforts to explain that his kingship is of a

categorically different kind than that which concerns Pilate, the
Roman does not catch the point of Jesus' words. His only conclusion
is that Jesus does purport to be some sort of a king. Jesus' response
that his kingship is concerned with the Truth leads the cautious,
political animal to ask cynically, "What is truth?"—again without the
slightest notion of the meaning of Jesus' words.

Scene three (18:38b–40) finds Pilate confronting the crowd again. It
is obvious that he has made Jesus' kingship the real issue. No charge
has been voiced up to now, but Pilate speaks of Jesus as the "king of
the Jews." Pilate tries compromise. "You may select one prisoner to
be freed as an expression of the graciousness of Rome. Surely you
want Jesus released." His compromising solution is rejected, and he
is sent back into the chambers more concerned now than before. His
attempt to resolve the situation through compromise suggests that he
understands the power of this mob.

In scene four (19:1–3), still hoping for compromise, Pilate has Jesus
tortured and mocked. This short scene implies that we are seeing an
increasingly desperate Pilate, as he tries to find a way of consoling the
crowd while still maintaining the pretense of his authority over these
dismal people.

The scene with Pilate and Jesus yields to another encounter with
the crowd—scene five (19:4–7). Pilate declares that Jesus is innocent
but shows the crowd he has punished Jesus and makes fun of his
kingship. But this compromise is no more effective than the first, and
now the crowd cries out for Jesus' crucifixion. The increasing anxiety
of Pilate is paralleled by the swelling demand of the crowd. Pilate is
more honest now—he cannot find reason to condemn Jesus. "He is
no king. If you want him dead, do it yourself." Now suddenly the
crowd voices a new charge, one that has not been expressed until
now: Jesus must die, for he claims to be the Son of God! John has now
successively moved away the façades to get at the real truth. The
truth is that humanity cannot endure the confrontation with the divine. It is then really a religious matter, not a political one at all. But
that is only partially correct. The real charge is that the accused is one
who undermines both the religious and the political establishments.
The kingship Jesus claims for himself is far more dangerous to Rome
than any claim to political power. John's crowd is saying that the

world of darkness and unbelief, the world that attempts to maintain itself apart from any dependence on the divine, cannot tolerate the presence of one who dissolves all authority and all powers.

Scene six (19:8–11): Pilate is now frightened. His abhorrence of the crowd, his anxiety to resolve this issue without compromising his image of authority, is transformed into terror. And without knowing it he now asks the *right* question: "Where do you come from?" Jesus' origin is what is really at stake, although Pilate does not realize the poignancy with which he has spoken. Jesus' composure is not shaken by all of this, and he remains silent before Pilate's question. The terrified Pilate threatens Jesus with his pseudoauthority. "I have the power of life and death over you. You had better listen!" (Pilate's words resemble those of a little child whose tearful threat speaks more of broken pride than of reality.) Jesus reminds Pilate of what the Roman had only vaguely understood until now, namely, that his authority is derivative and not absolute; and now he stands before the one who is the source of that derived authority.

Scene seven (19:12): Pilate's last effort to escape the ever-tightening jaws of this nightmarish situation results only in the final word from the crowd (v. 12). In what constitutes Pilate's fourth effort to mitigate the crowd, he is struck with the final blow. Until now it has been unspoken, but here in the shortest of the scenes in this powerful act the crowd says what Pilate has been fearing all along. If Pilate allows this one who insinuates political authority to himself by his claim to divine authority to go free, then Pilate has taken a stand against Caesar. The crowd knows this fear and that it will put the Roman governor at their mercy. They need only report to the powers in Rome: A representative of the empire has tolerated a subversive in their midst, and Pilate's career is ended, and perhaps even his life.

The concluding eighth scene (19:13–16) brings the three parties together a second time (compare 19:4). Taking his official position as Rome's judge in this land, Pilate presents the crowd with "their king." Pilate has been subdued. He accepts the fabricated charge and calls Jesus their king. "But are you sure you want him put to death?" The crowd will settle for nothing less. The last dastardly act of the crowd is to declare their loyalty to the Roman emperor. And with that declaration the trial of humanity which had begun with Jesus' appearance before Annas is concluded. Confronted with the choices of

loyalty to their Creator and loyalty to the worldly power of Rome,
they have chosen the latter. Their distortion of authority and power is
complete. John brings this moving scene to a climax with the declaration of the loyalty of the crowd, but he puts the sentencing of Jesus in
context with an unobtrusive reference to the time of day (v. 14). Noon
of the day before Passover was the time to slay the Passover lambs
and prepare them for the evening meal. As those lambs are prepared,
Jesus is about to be executed.

Pilate's anxiety and worried efforts to avoid a confrontation with
the crowd have increased to a near frenzy. The crowd's emotional
demand for the death of Jesus has mounted with each scene to an
impassioned vehemence which climaxes in their confession of
idolatrous loyalty. Throughout these eight scenes, alternating Pilate's
attention between the crowd and Jesus, the composure of Jesus has
been the sole constant. While Pilate and the crowd have struggled
with one another over the fate of this man, his own posture has been
that of a quiet and unperturbed monarch. The crowd and the governor
think that they are deliberating the fate of this Jesus, but it is obvious
that his fate is determined elsewhere than in this frenzied earthly
encounter.

What does John want us to make of the figure of Pilate? Surely, for
John, Pilate represents one whose loyalty is ultimately attached to his
own well-being. He struggles to avoid the sentence of death for Jesus
not because he is committed to justice but because he does not want to
impugn his own status. Pilate represents the whole of humanity,
trying to deal with this revealer of God without loss of earthly security
and authority.

THE CRUCIFIXION AND BURIAL (19:17–42)

The trial before Pilate has already explained the crucifixion. Humanity is trying to rid itself of this haunting notion that God's truth is
other than what we would like it to be. The cross is the final act of the
world in darkness to overcome the light which has, uninvited, cast its
beams into the human realm (1:5).

Jesus carries his own cross to the place of the execution—for John,
an act that symbolizes Jesus' sovereign role in the crucifixion. Jesus is
nailed to the cross between two others. But above the head of Jesus

stands the announcement, "Jesus of Nazareth, the King of the Jews," written by Pilate in three languages, encompassing the whole of the known world! The religious leaders are uneasy with this, as well they might be, and so they beg Pilate to revise it. But the ironic confession of faith is left as it is written. Pilate, unknowingly, expresses the real meaning of the crucifixion. The true monarch of humanity is being enthroned. Paradoxically the act by which humanity has tried to rid itself of the one who claims to be from God is the very act that exalts him upon his throne.

Psalm 22 is subtly and quietly used as the filter through which one is invited to read this account of the crucifixion (19:24). The soldiers gamble for the seamless robe they have taken from the victim, a further mockery of his status. At the foot of the cross stand the only followers courageous enough to witness publicly to their allegiance to Jesus—his mother, his aunt, Mary Magdalene, and the unnamed disciple whom John identifies only as the disciple Jesus especially loved. The first of three statements spoken by Jesus from the cross is addressed to that disciple and to his mother. In an act of love and concern, the dying Jesus commissions the beloved disciple with the care of his mother.

Jesus' sovereign lordship, even in the midst of his suffering, is never compromised. He knows that this is the final, fulfilling act of the revelation of God, and it is from this perspective that he participates in the hour. To fulfill Scripture, although it is not clear which passage John has in mind here, Jesus speaks of his thirst. He is offered wine and accepts it. Then he speaks the words he has yearned to utter: "It is finished." His suffering and death is the final act by which Jesus remains faithful to his Father. What is finished in Jesus' death is God's plan by which the divine love he has expressed in Christ is enthroned in a supreme deed of love, which means the exaltation of Christ as Lord and King.

The concern of 19:31–37 is a new theme in the narrative John has been unfolding. He wants us to know with certainty that Jesus did actually die. Lest the emphasis upon Jesus' sovereign lordship through the crucifixion be mistaken to mean that the death of Jesus was only a pretense, John assures us of the genuineness of the death experience. The religious leaders are in a hurry to clear up this whole messy affair before Sabbath should begin with the setting of the sun.

Breaking the legs, and sometimes additional bones, of the victims of crucifixion was a means of hastening death. That Jesus' legs are not broken because he is already dead has a double meaning. First, it assures us readers that Jesus is *actually* dead, and, second, it is another fulfillment of Scripture for the evangelist (v. 36). The reality of Jesus' death is affirmed again by the thrust of the spear into the side and the issuance of blood and water from the wound. Finally, John confirms the death of Jesus by asserting that the account is based on an eyewitness (v. 35).

The short but emphatic statement of Jesus' death is followed by his burial. Two men whose allegiance to Jesus has been a closely guarded secret come forward to take care of the body and hence come "out of the closet" with their faith. A man of apparent wealth, Joseph of Arimathea, and Nicodemus ask and gain permission to take the body. They prepare it for burial with the proper embalming spices and linen wrappings. In a nearby tomb they lay the body. Its "final" resting place is appropriate for a king, for it is a new tomb, one never before used. And that is that, or so they think.

John's carefully constructed account of the death and burial of Jesus spans an immense chasm, stretched tightly in order to touch both sides. On the one side, Jesus is not at all a victim, not at all the poor humiliated prophet thrust into horrible circumstances beyond his control. Rather, Jesus is the royal figure, majestically striding through his enthronement. But on the other side of this immeasurable chasm is the *reality of his death experience*. John would not allow us to think that this crucifixion has been a well-orchestrated sham. Jesus' death is real. His death has to be real in order for the exaltation of the King to be real. He makes the incongruiȳ inescapable: The loving death for others enthrones the King. He is "lifted up."

THE DISCOVERY OF
THE EMPTY TOMB (20:1-10)

Coming out of the darkness of this world, Mary Magdalene goes to the tomb. Amid the bleak portrayal of humanity, this Mary stands as one of John's models for what it means to believe. When she finds the stone rolled away from the opening of the tomb, she concludes that the body of her Lord has been stolen. She runs to inform the disciples, and Peter along with the beloved disciple dash to the tomb to see for themselves. Peter is left behind by the beloved disciple who reaches the tomb first, but then (out of courtesy to Peter?) waits and allows Peter to enter the tomb first. Peter enters, sees the burial clothes there but no body, and walks in a daze from the tomb. The beloved disciple then enters, sees the same thing Peter had seen, and believes that his master has risen from the tomb (although he did not yet fully understand what had taken place, John adds). Pondering what had happened, the disciples return to their home, leaving Mary alone at the tomb.

John tells the story of the empty tomb as if it is another of the "signs" done by Jesus. Like the wonder of changing the water into wine or the feeding of the multitude, the empty tomb is an event to which the disciples are forced to respond. And like the other signs, this one is ambiguous. Peter can perceive the facts of the empty tomb and go away puzzled, while the beloved disciple beholds the same thing and from it ventures to believe that Jesus is again alive. On the first level then the crucifixion and resurrection of Jesus constitute a final "sign" that evokes and invites faith. Only those with the courage to believe amid the unbelief and uncertainty of the world can see in this grand sign the workings of the Father. But there is still another level to which John will lead us before he concludes his discussion of faith and resurrection.

THE APPEARANCES OF THE
RESURRECTED JESUS (20:11–29)

While the empty tomb evoked the faith of the beloved disciple, that faith could not yet be mature Easter faith, for there was still awaiting the faithful an opportunity to know the resurrected Christ. John gives Mary Magdalene the privilege of the first appearance story (20:11–18). Mary has been left at the empty tomb and stands there weeping, for she is sure that someone has desecrated the tomb of her master. She looks into the tomb, as had Peter and the beloved disciple, and sees there two angels who ask her the reason for her tears. They do not inform her of the resurrection, however, for she is about to experience that firsthand.

She does not immediately recognize the resurrected Christ but mistakes him for the gardener. It is not until Jesus speaks her name that she realizes it is her Lord to whom she speaks. She is promptly told not to hold (or cling) to him, for he has not yet completed the process of returning to his Father. She is asked to go to the disciples and inform them that he has risen and is returning to his Father. Mary obediently does as her Lord has commanded.

Each of John's accounts of resurrection appearances is filled with his own special sense of the meaning of the crucifixion. It is Mary's sorrow that is so prominent at first. Then that sorrow is transformed. As the shepherd knows his sheep by name (10:3), it is her name uttered by the resurrected Christ that opens her eyes. The risen Christ names his believers, giving them their identity as his followers. Then Mary is given a job to do, which she obediently fulfills. Jesus' ascension, which is alluded to in v. 17, is for John an integral part of the crucifixion and resurrection, and not a separable movement in itself. It is, in other words, not an event in time but one of the several meanings of the death and resurrection of Jesus.

The second of the resurrection appearances is told succinctly in 20:19–23. As the first appearance occurred in the midst of Mary's sorrow, so the second is couched in the context of the disciples' fear (v. 19). John seems to suggest that the resurrected Christ comes to believers where they are imprisoned by their own shortsighted emotions. Jesus appears among his disciples and greets them in a typical manner, "Peace be with you." As he had identified himself to Mary with the sound of his voice, among his disciples he now assures them that he is none other than their master who had died on the cross. Jesus shows them the signs of his crucifixion. Their fear is transformed into joy by the presence of their risen Lord, and again Jesus bestows his peace upon them (v. 21; see 14:27 and 16:22).

After the joyful recognition of her Lord, Mary is commissioned to inform others of his presence. So now the disciples, joyful over their encounter with the risen Christ, are commissioned. They are sent forth, even as Jesus was sent into the world by the Father (19:21). They are empowered for their mission with the Holy Spirit which is the wind of the divine presence now transmitted in the breath of the risen Son. The Holy Spirit empowers them for their mission and equips them to forgive and withhold forgiveness on behalf of the Father (vv. 22–23). Their solemn commissioning completed, it is implied that Jesus departs from their midst.

In John's understanding of the resurrection appearances there is a double-faceted experience involved. On the one hand, there is a transformation of condition for those graced with the presence of the risen Christ—sorrow to joy and fear to joy. But John suggests in these stories that the gift of the resurrection appearance always carries with it a mission. In the case of the appearance to the disciples in the closed room it is the weighty mission of the community of faith to mediate forgiveness available in Christ. But there is a third appearance story which climaxes John's trilogy.

Thomas, the Twin, had the misfortune not to be present when the risen Christ had appeared to the disciples. His response to the reports of that experience was one of utter disbelief. He is not about to base his belief on the experience of the others, and he insists on a direct experience of the resurrected Lord if he is to believe. Mary was in sorrow, the disciples in fear, and Thomas in doubt. To transform that doubt, the resurrected Christ appears again among the disciples, this time with Thomas present. Thomas is invited to touch the resurrected Christ, to feel the nail holes in his hands and the spear opening in his side. It was a firsthand experience Thomas wanted; it is a firsthand experience Thomas is given. His response is a confession of faith: "My Lord and my God!" His confession is accepted but modified with a beatitude: "Blessed are those who do not see (as you have seen) and yet believe (as you now believe)."

The resurrection appearances are the climactic conclusion of John's story of Jesus, and the appearance to Thomas in particular brings the Gospel to its peak of intensity and power. Two points are worth mentioning. First, in the climactic confession of Thomas, "My Lord and my *God*," we are brought full circle back to the prologue. John begins his Gospel with the daring confession that Jesus is God (1:1) and now closes his story of Jesus with a repetition of that confession.

Second, the last words spoken by Jesus in the Gospel proper (excluding for now the ending that we find in chapter 21) are a declaration that while believing on the basis of what one has seen is blessed, it is even more blessed to believe without the benefit of having seen. The faith which has arisen throughout the Gospel has been a faith that found roots in what was seen and experienced firsthand, as in Thomas's case. But now John speaks to his readers who have never had and would never have the privilege of a firsthand experience with Jesus as did the disciples of the Gospel. At the climax of his Gospel John says that those who dare to believe without the benefit of the experience of seeing Jesus are even more blessed than those chosen few who were eyewitnesses to the historical act of God in Christ. The barriers to faith are torn down by Thomas's experience with the resurrected Christ; now others are invited to overcome those barriers without the extraordinary gift of a resurrection appearance.

The trilogy of resurrection appearances testifies, in John's scheme of the passion story, to the fact that Jesus has been given the glory of God as none other. The exaltation of the King on the cross is completed with his return to the Father.

SUMMARY

John's passion story leads the reader through a number of moods, as we have noticed. We began with a strong sense of the judgment of humans occurring in what was being done with Jesus. The strongly judgmental flavor of the early portions of the narrative, however, are balanced, now that we can look back over the whole, with the good news of what Jesus' death and resurrection do for humanity. In the resurrection scenes we have witnessed John's demonstration of how the dying and rising Christ transforms human existence. John sees the cross as both judgment and redemption.

His passion story pivots, however, around two related points: First, Jesus is the sovereign Lord even throughout his passion; that point has been inescapable in the narrative. The second, and related to this point, is that the cross and resurrection are for John the glorification of Jesus. In the passion, as John understands it, God gives Jesus glory and "lifts him up" to his rightful place as King and Lord. This is understandable only if we recognize that what leads Jesus to the cross is the *unlimited love of the Father for all humanity* (the "world," according to 3:16). The most extreme, the highest expression of love—"laying down" one's life for friends—glorifies that love and enthrones it as the highest meaning life can have.

So now the two focal points of John's narrative are enmeshed. Jesus reveals glory and receives glory. The two, of course, are one and the same. Jesus can reveal glory because he has received glory; and he receives glory because he has so faithfully revealed it in his life and work. John would have us end his story of Jesus with one sure conviction: It is in the person of Jesus that we humans find ourselves in contact with the divine glory itself, that is, in contact with God abiding in our midst.

Conclusion:
Endings

20:30—21:25

When we first began our investigation of John's story of Jesus, we were met with the narrator's love of *beginnings*. We first encountered a "cosmic" beginning *and* then a "historical" beginning. Perhaps then we should be prepared for what appears to be John's love of *endings* as well! For, as he concludes the story of Jesus, he ends not once, but twice. Those responsible for the Gospel had one excellent ending when they devised another excellent ending and, not wanting to choose among them, included them both! The two endings, in fact, enhance the power of the Gospel and complete the story of Jesus in a masterful way.

CONCLUSION NUMBER ONE (20:30–31)

Here in but two simple sentences is a profound conclusion to John's story of Jesus. The author wants us to know, first of all, that the story he has told is not at all complete. There are many other things Jesus did that gave expression to the presence of God—"signs" in the sense that word is used in the Gospel.

Having told us something about his story (its incompleteness), John now gives us the *reason* for the story. Its purpose is singular and noble: It is designed to help the reader believe that this Jesus is none other than what he has claimed to be, Messiah and Son of God. Whether the reader's faith is as new and fresh as the story itself or whether it spans a whole lifetime, this story is told to strengthen and nourish that faith. But the story has as its goal not only the nurturing of faith but also the fostering of the consequences of that faith, namely, life. John hopes this story will nourish faith and the fruit of faith which is genuine life, life as the Creator intended it. John has spoken many times of this quality of existence that is authentic human life, and he has called it by many different names: eternal life, abundant life, truth, light, and so forth. But here in his conclusion he speaks of it with the simplest of expressions. God wants humans to believe in the revelation of his presence in Christ in order that they might LIVE. So for John the goal of his story of Jesus is that we ourselves might believe and consequently live!

It is no surprise that John tells his story with more in mind than the delight of hearing another good story! That is perhaps reason enough for any story. But it is by stories that we orient ourselves in this world; stories help us understand who we are and what we are for. John's story of Jesus is the pristine story that puts us in contact with our original nature. This story is more than another tale—it is THE story by which our whole existence is given structure and meaning. As we enter into this story, we are changed and enlarged into creatures put back into relationship with their Creator. Thus is John's understanding of the purpose of his story.

THE SIGN OF THE WONDROUS CATCH OF FISH: EIGHTH SIGN? (21:1–14)

From the grandeur of life and faith to a story of a fishing trip! The setting for the story takes us back to where we were in the middle of chapter 20. This is going to be another story of a resurrection appearance (21:1), only this time we are back in Galilee, back on Lake Tiberius—back home for the disciples. Seven of the disciples are gathered together, and Peter declares that he is going fishing—a strange act given the character of the events that have just transpired, but then let us remember that these disciples may have been fishermen by trade. So, fishing they did go, but with little success. All night long they have been at it, but with absolutely no luck. As the sun is rising, a strange figure appears on the shore and asks them how the fishing has been this morning. After they have reported their failure, not easy for seasoned fishermen to admit, the stranger instructs them to throw their net on the other side of the boat. They do so and instantly their net is filled to overflowing with fish—shortly, we will learn, one hundred and fifty-three big ones (v. 11). The beloved disciple then recognizes who the stranger is, or dares for the first time to say who he thought it was all along, and tells Peter, "It's our Lord!" Brave, eager, not-always-wise Peter immediately wraps his coat around him and dives in to swim to shore. When the boat finally arrives at the shore, pulling its bounteous catch of fish, Jesus is waiting there for them with a blazing fire, fish, and bread. Taking some of the fish from their bloated net, Jesus cooks breakfast and feeds his disciples again. The disciples are so dumbfounded by the whole thing that they sit in silence, unable to think of anything to say worthy of the occasion.

John has added to his resurrection appearances a combination resurrection appearance *and* sign story. It unites the stories of the wondrous deeds of Jesus told earlier in the Gospel with the resurrection appearances narrated in chapter 20. Like the other resurrection stories this one affirms once again the way in which the resurrected Christ transforms the human condition. This time the condition of need and failure is turned into a condition of plenty and fellowship. With this transformation of the human condition we are again linked up with an earlier story in the Gospel. The feeding of the multitude (6:1-15), which was so clearly a revelation of God's glory in Christ, is now repeated in a resurrection setting (21:1-14). As the historical Jesus went about filling human need and overpowering want, so the resurrected Christ goes on doing that same thing among those who have the courage to identify him as the one standing nearby to help.

PETER'S REINSTATEMENT (21:15–19)

The resurrection appearance John has just narrated has another purpose, however. Poor Peter, brave and committed, was nonetheless the victim of his own human weakness. John does not want us to forget that, and he does not want us to think that Jesus forgot it either. The resurrected Christ now transforms the human condition of that one who had earlier failed him.

Jesus asks Peter no less than *three times* if Peter loves him. Three times Peter answers in the affirmative, feeling more and more despondent because Jesus goes on asking him in spite of his answers. In response to each of Peter's answers, Jesus commands Peter to care for the sheep. (The rhythmic quality of the conversation in English hides the fact that in the Greek the vocabulary varies with each of the exchanges: two different words for love are used.) Jesus seems to be asking if, in every way possible, Peter will love him and, in a variety of ways, care for his sheep.

John jogs our memories and asks us to think back to that dreadful scene in the courtyard of Annas when Peter is asked *three times* if he is not one of the disciples of Jesus and three times denies his association with the one on trial. That is, John wants us to read this present narrative in the light of Peter's threefold denial (18:12–27). Peter is asked three times to affirm his love for Jesus and to commit himself to the care of all of those who would come to believe in the Father's Son. Resurrection signifies the overcoming of those failures of human faith and their assignment to the past once and for all. John could not end his story of Jesus without telling how Peter experienced his own resurrection from the tomb of dreadful failure. But like the other resurrection appearances, Peter's reinstatement brings not only the grace of forgiveness but also the call to mission—care for the sheep.

With the threefold confession completed (21:17), Jesus informs Peter of his role in the revelation of God's glory. His freedom and self-determination will be taken from him, as well as his life. All of this, John tells us in an aside, is to help readers understand the way in which Peter would witness to his Christ—in bondage and death as well as in freedom and service. This brief section ends with the words Peter had doubtlessly first heard in his initial contact with Jesus, "Follow me." The discipleship to which Peter was first called (1:35–42) is reaffirmed now by the resurrected Christ. Peter will follow Jesus in service and then in faithful death.

THE DISCIPLE JESUS LOVED (21:20–24)

Often we have seen the mysterious disciple whom Jesus loved appear in John's narrative in connection with Peter (for example, 13:23–24). Now we find them again connected in this closing scene of the Gospel. If Peter has been restored by the resurrected Christ, the beloved disciple is destined by the resurrected Christ. Peter asks about the beloved disciple, and Jesus assures Peter that this special disciple will live until Christ comes. Apparently John must relate this little incident in order that we not misunderstand the role of the beloved disciple, for he assures us that Jesus did *not* promise that the beloved disciple would never die but only that he would live until Christ came again. Christ has come again in this resurrection appearance, and so the destiny of the beloved disciple, like Peter's, is to die in faithfulness to his Lord.

But now in 21:24 we find the reason John has given such attention to this special disciple. It is he, John tells us, who is responsible for this story. It is he, the beloved disciple, who first told this story and perhaps even wrote it. John's retelling of the story affirms that the testimony of the disciple Jesus loved was indeed true. So here in the closing paragraphs of his Gospel the narrator is disclosing to the reader the basis of his story. He would not want us to go away from our engagement in his story without knowing his indebtedness to the disciple he calls "the one Jesus loved."

CONCLUSION NUMBER TWO (21:25)

We arrive at the end—once again. John again tells us that there is more left to be said. As a matter of fact, if it all were told, it would take countless books to contain it. The story of Jesus is not completed, you see. What John has written is but a drop in the mighty sea of the Jesus story. In chapters 20 and 21 he had begun to recall those occasions on which the resurrected Christ made his transforming presence known. As he appeared and transformed the condition of Mary, the disciples in the locked room, Thomas, the seven unsuccessful fishermen, and the unfaithful Peter, so he continues to appear and transform human lives. It is those "other things that Jesus did" that the evangelist wants us to know about but that he can in no way narrate in any completeness.

SUMMARY

As we began to relive the story of Jesus as John tells it, it was suggested that John's story does not need interpretation as much as it needs simply to be heard. That story has a power in and of itself. We did not want to distract from it by telling it once again. If there is a

single thing that our journey through the pages of the Gospel of John
has accomplished, we hope that you the readers have perceived the
intrinsic power in John's story itself. A friend and colleague in a
church choir has a favorite expression: "This anthem will *sing itself,*
if we will just let it!" Good music is not sung as much as it is allowed to
sing us. A good story is not retold as much as it tells itself through us.
John's story was first told in order that the good news of God's act in
Christ might be expressed and reexpressed—generation after generation. That story has been preserved throughout the ages because, as it
told itself, it brought its hearers into the presence of God's untiring
love for humanity. Here it has been retold one more time for only one
objective—that it might retell itself for its divine purpose.